IN THE NAME OF ALLAH,
THE BENEFICENT, THE MERCIFUL

SAUDI ARABIA:
A KINGDOM IN TRANSITION

published by

**The Saudi Arabian Cultural Mission
to the
United States of America**

Editor

Dr. Abdulaziz I. Al-Sweel

Assistant Editors

Richard Bianchi

Andrew Evans

Printed in the United States of America

10 9 8 7 6 5 4 3 2 1

ISBN 0-915957-14-6

AMANA PUBLICATIONS
10710 Tucker Street
Beltsville, MD 20705
Tel: (301) 595-5777
Fax: (301) 595-5888

Introducing Saudi Arabia

Introducing Saudi Arabia is a series of publications, written, edited, presented and distributed by the Saudi Arabian Cultural Mission to the United States of America.

The purpose of this series is to enhance the understanding and friendship between people of other nationalities and Saudi Arabians, to present our history, culture, religion, government and society. These books will provide individuals and organizations with accurate and up to date information about the dynamics of the Kingdom of Saudi Arabia.

To receive a complimentary copy of this publication and other materials about Saudi Arabia please contact:

Saudi Arabian Cultural Mission
Information & Cultural Affairs Department
2600 Virginia Avenue, N.W.
Washington, D.C. 20037

ACKNOWLEDGEMENTS

The editors would like to thank the many people who helped with the organization of this book. Our deepest gratitude goes to H.R.H. Prince Bandar Bin Sultan Bin Abdulaziz, Saudi Arabia's Ambassador to the United States, who was both encouraging and supportive of our work on this text. We would like to extend our appreciation to Dr. Hamad I. Al-Salloom, the Saudi Arabian Cultural Attache to the United States and to Mr. Abdulrahman Al-Dayel, Director of Cultural Affairs and Dr. Abdulmohsen Al-Helal, Associate Director for Cultural Affairs, for providing exceptional resources and additional suggested reading materials from the Saudi Arabian Cultural Missions' Resource Center.

As for the book itself, we want all of the contributors, readers and reviewers to know how much their work is appreciated. We would especially like to express our gratitude to Dr. Sheila Scoville, Dr. Barbara Bryant and Dr. J.W. Wright, for their comments and revisions. Furthermore, we would like to acknowledge the contribution of Dr. Fahad Al-Nasser, from the Islamic Section of the Royal Embassy of Saudi Arabia. The time and effort devoted by Clayton Westland to an earlier version of this text is greatly appreciated. Finally, our editors at Amana Corporations deserve our thanks for helping with the layout of this book.

TABLE OF CONTENTS

BASIC FACTS (1991 statistics unless otherwise indicated)

Area: 839,996 square miles (one-third the size of the U.S.)

Capital city: Riyadh (estimated population 1,800,000 in 1991)

Other major cities: Jiddah (estimated population 1,500,000 in 1991),
Makkah (estimated population 630,000 in 1991)

Population: 15,431,000 (estimated)

Population density: 15 per square mile

Life expectancy at birth: 65

Total fertility rate (births per woman): 7

Physicians: 1 per 852 persons

Hospital beds: 1 per 406 persons

School enrollment: 60%

Illiteracy rate: 46%

Gross national product: $105,133,000,000 (1989)

GNP per capita: $7,070 (1990)

Daily calorie supply per capita: 2,874

Arable land: 2%

Acres under cultivation: 7,400,000 (1992)

Agriculture's share in GNP: 7.3% (1989)

Average rainfall: 2-4 inches; 20 inches in Asir province

Principal crops: Dates, wheat, barley, fruit

Minerals: Oil, gas, gold, copper, iron

Crude oil reserves: 255,000,000,000 barrels

Industries: Petrochemicals

Labor force: (1990) 9.9% agriculture; 6.5% manufacturing; 53%
services, commerce; 10.8% government; 16.4% construction

Foreign trade: Imports (1991): $47,850,000,000; 16.7% from U.S.;
15.3% from Japan; 11.3% from United Kingdom
Exports (1991): $29,112,000,000; 24% to U. S.; 19% to Japan

National budget (1992): $48,000,000,000

Share of GNP spent on defense: 30% (1992)

Monetary unit: Riyal; 3.745 riyals = US $1 (June 1992)

Source: The World Bank Atlas, 25th anniversary edition (1992); *The World Almanac and Book of Facts 1992; Saudi Arabia Country Profile 1992-93.*

LIST OF TABLES

LIST OF FIGURES

Page

MAPS

INTRODUCTION

by
Hamad Al-Salloom, Ph.D.
Cultural Attache to the U.S.A.

To the American public, the Kingdom and people of Saudi Arabia remain somewhat an unknown and little understood nation and population. Yet, the United States and the Kingdom of Saudi Arabia share what many consider to be one of the greatest mutually beneficial relationships ever forged, encompassing many international spheres of interest. The mass mobilization of U.S. troops in Saudi Arabia during the Gulf War has produced an unprecedented influence on the American population, affecting the public towards the desire for knowledge and a greater understanding of the Kingdom and people of Saudi Arabia.

As the world grows more interdependent, the Kingdom of Saudi Arabia has the desire to be understood and to develop a legitimate educational interest in this long observed, yet veiled land of princes, desert and petroleum. There are a great number of publications about Saudi Arabia, yet many of these works are not within easy access to mass audiences around the country. The Royal Embassy of Saudi Arabia's Cultural Mission in Washington, D.C. has moved to the forefront in providing and in distributing information to the American public. We seek to fulfill this opportunity to educate the curious audience with materials regarding the unique and distinctive characteristics of Saudi Arabian history, politics, education, economics and society.

This book seeks to present a comprehensive view of the many facets of the Kingdom of Saudi Arabia. The Saudi Arabian Cultural Mission possesses great academic resources to provide an expansive amount of information pertaining to Saudi Arabia. During the course of the next few months we will be compiling this information to provide the American population with several more specific books that offer an in depth panorama of a country that has recently achieved prominent world wide political, economic and social status. This book touches upon the many fascinating events and institutions that have shaped Islam, the political geography of the Arabian Peninsula, Saudi economic policy and social structure.

"Saudi Arabia: A Kingdom In Transition," attempts to provide you, the reader, with a glimpse into the Arab-Islamic world of Saudi Arabia. Saudi Arabia is a nation and population founded upon strong religious values and deep Arabian pride, nevertheless as the title expounds, Saudi Arabia is a land that is not immune from the modernization and advances of the twentieth century and beyond. Therefore, we too search for our role in the political, economic and social climate of tomorrow. Rest assured, the Kingdom of Saudi Arabia will remain firmly grounded upon the religious values of Islam and the deep seated regard for family. Above all, we hope that you will enjoy reading this book and gain a greater understanding of the Kingdom of Saudi Arabia.

Map 1
Map of the Kingdom of Saudi Arabia

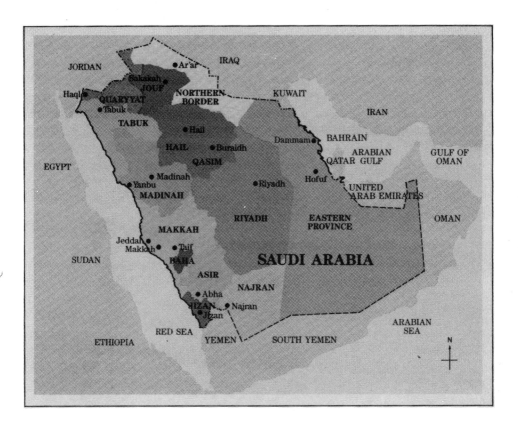

Chapter 1
SAUDI ARABIA TODAY

The Arabian desert—sunbaked, endlessly wind-scoured, pitted and pocked, slashed by rocky limestone cliffs and rounded by drifting sand—stretches immense across beds of impermeable rock, beneath which an ancient sedimentary basin traps huge pockets of oil. Even the sea off the eastern coast of the Arabian Peninsula ebbs and flows above vast reservoirs of precious petroleum.

Countries in this region—Iran, Iraq, and the small Gulf states—share this huge accumulation of hydrocarbons, but none to the extent of Saudi Arabia. Within the space of three decades, oil wealth has transformed a somnolent web of nomadic herdsmen leading their camels from oasis to oasis into a network of brightly-lit modern cities, connected by broad highways to oil refineries, pipeline pump stations, and petrochemical complexes.

The images of Saudi Arabia that have lodged in the Western mind are a confused mixture of fact and fable. They begin with a residue of tales from *The Thousand and One Nights*, heard in childhood, and add illusions from stereotyped movies and television programs that revolve around mysterious hidden treasures, magic genies, and glittering palaces, where veiled women dance behind pierced screens, while incense perfumes the air and jewels glitter in the flicker of hanging lamps. Another image is of thousands of white-clad pilgrims crowding an ancient mosque in Makkah (Mecca). Other fragmented memories summon up an oil embargo resulting in long lines at American gas stations, and a Saudi astronaut, Prince Sultan bin Salman al Saud, who rode the space shuttle *Discovery* in 1985.

Then, nightly television in the second half of 1990 brought into American living-rooms vast moonscapes of rock and sand, swirling in blinding clouds of dust. The focus was on the half-million young American servicemen and women who spent six months camped in the heat and the grit, awed by that bleak, yet violent, landscape, drinking endless bottles of desalinated water to prevent dehydration.

Those electronic images gave Americans a feeling of apprehension, a sense of having a perilous stake in what was happening in that far-away desert. The coverage of that conflict is the only current picture most Americans have of Saudi Arabia. The soldiers who served there brought home a very limited glimpse of the reality, for they were far away from the centers of civilian population.

The thousands of American technicians and businessmen who have worked in Saudi Arabia during the last half-century have a far more accurate picture, but their expertise reaches a fairly narrow audience of family and friends when they return to the United States. We need to know a great deal more about this country that sits on top of a quarter of the world's petroleum reserves, if we are to deal intelligently with it in the future.

Privacy as Public Policy

Saudi Arabia is not an easy country to know and understand, because the Saudis are very private and protective of their cultural traditions. They do not want the outside world impinging in a way that would destroy their extraordinary cultural, religious, linguistic, and ethnic cohesion. No visas are issued for casual travel to Saudi Arabia. Frivolous tourists and curiosity seekers are not welcome. Foreigners entering the country must be engaged in legitimate tasks, of which the Saudis approve. Consequently, development analysts have gone to the country as advisers, rather than as researchers. Competent Saudis who might publish sociological descriptions of their country in English are generally too busy with implementing development plans to spend their time analyzing the intricacies of their society.

This protectiveness contributes, unfortunately, both to misinformation and to a dearth of accurate information outside the kingdom. One of the consequences of the Gulf War is a greater awareness among the Saudis that mutual trust among allies requires a large degree of mutual understanding, and conflicts in the Middle East are exacerbated by misconceptions on all sides. The need of the outside world for accurate and accessible information about Saudi Arabia, objectively analyzed, is gradually being recognized.

THE COUNTRYSIDE

The Red Sea and Gulf of Aden are part of the Great Rift Valley that runs south through Africa. Saudi Arabia sits beside the Red Sea on a platform, tilted, with bold high mountains in the west along the coast. Hijaz, the name of the province that blankets those rocky hills, means "barrier." The country slopes gradually downward toward the east until it stretches flat and low along the Gulf coast, which is fringed by extensive coral reefs. (The Arabians call the body of water to the east the "Arabian Gulf;" the Iranians call it the "Persian Gulf." Outsiders who prefer to offend no one call it simply "the Gulf.")

Saudi Arabia is the largest country in the world without a river. Rainfall is erratic, averaging two to four inches a year, except in the west and southwest. The mountains there can capture twenty inches during the annual monsoon, but even so, terraces are needed to trap and hold the precious moisture.

Most of the Kingdom lacks sufficient water for cultivation. Some regions are pocked by barren, stony outcroppings, the plains below cluttered with great boulders that have crashed down over the ages from the highlands. The Syrian desert in the north extends southward into the 22,000 square miles of the Al-Nafud desert. In the south of Saudi Arabia, the Rub al-Khali (called the "Empty Quarter" because it is uninhabitable), extends over 250,000 square miles. There, drifting sand, an accumulation of centuries of fierce gales blowing across empty landscape, with no green plant cover to break the wind's force or hold the soil in place, sifts in endless undulating ribbons and high ridges across fields of rock and flat, white plains. Intense heat in the interior often exceeds 110 degrees Fahrenheit, yet the temperature can dip below freezing at night.

Before irrigation was available, perhaps only 150,000 acres of land in Saudi Arabia was cultivated, mostly in the traditional oases with their date palms. Al Hasa Oasis in the Eastern Province is the largest such oasis in the world. In it, grew thousands of date palms, which provided food, wood for fires, and leaves for roof thatch and baskets. Saudi Arabia still produces half-a-million tons of dates annually.

Water as a Crucial Resource

By 1992, farming had spread over 7,400,000 acres in the Kingdom. Water has been the key. Spring water in oases has been funneled into efficient irrigation systems. New dams and reservoirs have been built to catch precious rainfall. Deep underground aquifers, trapped between layers of rock, have been tapped with artesian wells. Important aquifers have been located in central Saudi Arabia, permitting a large cattle-growing project east of the capital, at Haradh. Poultry and dairy farms now meet most local needs.

FLORA AND FAUNA

No desert is completely barren or empty. Even in the Empty Quarter, a good rain every three or four years is enough to sustain a particularly hardy species of salt grass, which provides fodder for the single-humped dromedary camel. The Bedouin drive their beasts from water hole to water hole, traveling twenty or thirty miles a day, and the camels drink thirty gallons of water at once, to sustain them through the long trek to the next oasis. Their masters drink camel milk to survive through the long, waterless days.

Other animals can also live in the desert because of their ability to run swiftly and cover long distances: two types of antelope, foxes, wolves, hyenas, wildcats, cheetahs, jackals. Burrowing animals thrive—hedgehogs, hares, reptiles, and lizards. Flamingos and pelicans are common where water is available, as are smaller birds in oases and shore birds along the coasts. Falcons provide hunting for enthusiastic Saudi sportsmen.

Only a few inches of rain cause a surprising amount of vegetation to green the landscape, mostly varieties which have narrow, spiny leaves—juniper, aloe, tamarisk—or are water-storing, like euphorbia and cacti. After even the lightest rainfall, the desert is painted almost overnight with drifts of green seedlings of fast-growing grasses, which mature rapidly and drop their hardy seeds to await the next rain. This ground cover provides seasonal grazing for camels, goats, cattle, and the swift Arabian horse so prized for racing.

The rainfall that seeps so rapidly through the porous desert sand is trapped in basins of rock. Where these bubble to the surface in springs, reeds grow in profusion and are used as thatch for houses.

Near Haradh, where one of the Kingdom's first experimental farms was established at Al Kharj in the late 1940s, huge irrigated fields of wheat, melons, potatoes, and market gardens stretch from horizon to horizon. A major wheat-growing area is also located in Qasim, 300 miles north of Riyadh. Saudi Arabia produced four million tons of wheat in 1991—2.5 million tons more than needed for domestic consumption.

Also to the north at Unaizah and Buraidah, barriers of tamarisk and eucalyptus trees bar drifting sand from an important farming area, where date palms and vegetable gardens provide food for people alongside alfalfa fields, which supply fodder for livestock. Orchards of citrus fruits, peaches, apricots, and pomegranates have been planted near grape vineyards. New projects have been started to grow fish in ponds and tanks.

To live comfortably, people, too, must have large amounts of water. Saudi Arabia has invested more money in desalinizing sea water than any other country in the world. Potable water is brought from the Gulf to Riyadh, 310 miles away. Medina receives drinking water from the Red Sea, and work is under way to provide the same to Makkah and Taif, as well as to Asir Province, so that the natural water supply there can be allocated completely to agriculture.

Survival in the Desert

Before the discovery of oil, the Arabian desert was not an environment that encouraged rugged individualism, particularly during long centuries of conquest and conflict, when Ottoman sultans were most interested in collecting tax revenues from pilgrims to Makkah. In that harsh landscape, single individuals were helpless, incapable of herding large flocks of livestock, or of moving food and water over long distances, or of merchandizing their goods in distant markets. Survival in the desert depended on close cooperation within the family or clan group that eked a meager living from herding animals from grassland to grassland after the scant rains or from harvesting dates in the scattered oases. Water and pasturage were never sufficient; competition for both was fierce. Extended family units tended their herds together, and fiercely defended their water and grazing rights. Burdens were distributed and shared as families followed their nomadic paths, with many pairs of hands working in tandem to shepherd the flocks of goats, load the camel caravans, and reach an oasis before food and water ran out.

Disputes were settled as every member of the group willingly participated in the execution of all decisions. Family groups gathered around their campfires to debate their courses of action, discussing their alternatives until consensus (*ijma* in Arabic) was achieved; then they looked to the acknowledged head of their group to execute the agreed plan.

Bedouin Heritage

Most of the Saudis are descended from nomads who ranged with the seasons, across the desert sands in search of water and grazing for their livestock. Organized into tribes, each tribe in turn, divided into many clans and subclans. Expansion of the power of any one tribe brought about the alliance of others in opposition to it. The tribes competed fiercely for the arid land's scarce resources. As many as 89 major Bedouin tribes have been identified in Saudi Arabia. They had a cohesive cultural tradition, precluding conflict over ideologies. Their lifestyle was open, egalitarian. Their shaykh (chief) was the first among equals. All spoke Arabic. All were Muslims.

Until the discovery of oil, the principal Saudi occupations were herding, fishing, pearl diving, and trading handicrafts. Only in the Hijaz were there commercial links with the outside world, which gave the urban Hijais a broader outlook than their desert cousins. The meager economy limited markets elsewhere; little economic surplus existed; the differences between rich and poor were slight. Land had no value as such to nomadic herdsmen; the Bedouin treasured their animals, the proud name they bore, and the honor of their clan.

The meteoric growth of the oil industry after World War II transformed the Bedouin way of life. To mute the competition among the tribes for water and grassland, King Abdul Aziz Ibn Saud had wells dug and encouraged permanent settlement of the nomads in farming villages, so that today only a small segment of the population moves from place to place with herds of livestock. The animals graze near pickup trucks, which very probably carried some of them from their previous encampment. In Bedouin tents generators power refrigerators and television sets.

THE GROWTH OF CITIES

The bulk of Saudi Arabia's oil wealth has been deliberately directed into social services, infrastructure, and economic enterprises designed to promote self-sustaining economic growth independent of crude oil production. Within the last two decades the implementation of these development plans has transformed a pastoral economy into a dynamic, modern society. Figures from the Ministry of Municipal and Rural Affairs indicate that 75 percent of Saudi Arabia's population now lives in cities, 22 percent lives in the country, and 3 percent is considered migratory.

The earliest modernization took place in the Hijaz, the most populous province, along the Red Sea, where education and administrative systems were first established. Urban Hijazis often sent their sons abroad for higher education. Plentiful employment attracted growing numbers of educated Arabs from other countries.

Because the Saudi government focused its attention on modernization, well-paid jobs and social services became readily available in the cities. The widening gap between rural and urban incomes brought a steady migration of population from the countryside to all the urban centers in Saudi Arabia. Most of the population shifted from livestock farming to oil production, construction, provision of services, and government bureaucracy—all urban activities. That migration introduced typical urban problems—unemployment, inadequate housing and social services, and a rising cost of living. The centers of power now are in the cities, rather than in the tribal-centered rural areas, and the function of cities has shifted from commerce to industry.

The growth of Saudi cities is a late 20th century phenomenon. Riyadh grew from 7,500 people in 1862 to 169,000 in 1962 to 1.8 million in 1991. Ras Tanura, begun in the late 1930s, has become the world's largest petroleum port. North of Ras Tanura a new industrial complex, Jubail, has risen out of the sands within a decade—as has Yanbu on the Red Sea coast. Both were constructed as part of Saudi Arabia's ambitious plans to develop hydrocarbon-based and energy-intensive industries as a route to self-sustaining growth.

The towns of Saudi Arabia have all the excitement of a new frontier. The streets bustle with vehicles of every description—limousines, taxis, chauffeured Mercedes, jeeps, vans, motorcycles. Heavy machinery seems to be constantly demolishing the old to make room for the new. Urban landscapes are a startling melange of skyscrapers, luxury hotels, gaudy palaces, imposing government office buildings, huge shopping centers blazing with neon signs, broad boulevards, clusters of modern villas all juxtaposed with the quaint, wooden- shuttered, and balconied facades of an earlier era. The empty lots of the 1970s, littered with rubble, construction cranes, and stacks of building materials, have been transformed into blocks of Moorish or modern architecture.

The excitement is generated by more than construction and a vast array of imported goods. There is also an atmosphere of vitality, of activity, of everyone being busy and involved. No weary-looking, apathetic bodies huddle on sidewalks or under trees with nothing to do, and no place to go, as is so common in many developing countries of the tropical world. No beggars assail the pedestrian, for jobs are available, and begging is against the law. Police apprehend panhandlers and take them to institutions to learn a skill and be put to work.

Modernity Manifested in Distinctive Public Architecture

The austere character of Islam in the Arabian Peninsula was reflected in the simplicity of its historic mosques—devoid of mosaics, marble, gardens, or other decorations. Even the mosques of Islam's holiest cities, Makkah and Medina, hidden in the folds of the western hills, are unostentatious, eschewing the decorative art forms used in many other Muslim countries. They reflect the depth of the kingdom's conservative religious convictions. When the call to prayer echoes from slender minarets, all activity stops in Saudi Arabia, a prayer rug or mat is laid down, and prayers are performed with a total lack of self-consciousness.

In the name of God, Most Gracious, Most Merciful. Praise be to God, the Cherisher and Sustainer of the Worlds; Most Gracious, Most Merciful; Master of the Day of Judgment. Thee do we worship, and Thine aid we seek. Show us the straight way, the way of those on whom Thou hast bestowed Thy Grace, Those whose (portion) is not wrath, and who go not astray.

Qur'an: I, 1-7

The vistas unfolded by the oil industry are as harsh as the surrounding desert. The many oil fields display endless grids of pipes and tanks and burning flares of gas. Uniform rows of workers' housing cluster around the many pump stations, bustling new port facilities, petrochemical complexes, and desalinization plants.

The harsh angularity of these utilitarian facilities contrasts sharply with the elegance of the public buildings constructed in urban centers. The new mosques, universities, government ministries, and airports display a continuity in design and feeling, a restraint that reflects the dimension and simplicity of the desert. Devoid of the gaudy colors, garish lighting, and complex fussiness of the royal palaces, these public buildings incorporate instead subtle contours, multiple arches, repeated parallel lines and curves, and richly diverse and textured materials, to achieve an understated elegance. Water, used in multiple fountains and pools, has a strong sensory appeal in the arid climate.

The contrasting sights and sounds and smells and textures of Saudi Arabia stir all the senses. The fragrance of incense and spices and coffee hangs over the markets. Shiny Cadillacs crowd long strings of camels pacing along the new highways. The muezzin's call to prayers echoes across the rooftops insistently through electronic amplification. In the country, every tree and overhang that provides shade becomes the site of holiday picnics for Saudi families.

Long coastlines are traced by intricate fish weirs in their shallows, where snorkelers browse over the coral reefs. Pristine beaches welcome picnickers, tuned to transistor radios, under bright beach umbrellas. Lateen-rigged fishing boats wend their lazy way past mammoth tankers loading fuel at submarine terminals offshore.

Amidst all these contrasts, an ancient, austere beauty illuminates the harsh and demanding landscape of Saudi Arabia. The people who live there are graced with an appealing warmth and serenity, strong convictions, and a determination to follow the path they have chosen. They deserve our understanding and good will.

King Abdul Aziz Bin Abdul Rahman Al-Saud,
founder of the modern Kingdom of Saudi Arabia

Chapter 2
THE ROLE OF ISLAM IN SAUDI ARABIA

In about 570 A.D., the Prophet of Islam was born in Arabia. His message would spread around the world and eventually embrace one-fifth of the human race. Muhammad lived in the ancient Arabian trading center called Makkah (Mecca), located around an important water source in the mountains that rise to the east of the Red Sea. Because he was a son of the soil of Arabia, the message presented by Muhammad is deeply embedded in the culture of the Saudi Kingdom, the political system he outlined is enshrined in its government, and its people take special pride in being the custodians of the holiest sites associated with the Muslim faith.

A similar (favour have ye already received) in that We have sent you an Apostle of your own, rehearsing to you Our Signs, and sanctifying you, and instructing you in Scripture and Wisdom, and in new Knowledge.

Qur'an: II, 151

The Arabian Peninsula in Antiquity

Arabia takes its name from its inhabitants, the Arabs. Before the time of the Prophet Muhammad, Arabs lived only in the Arabian Peninsula, which was populated then by many separate and distinct tribes, each worshipping particular deities.

Those earlier people, of course, had their own history. Archeologists have found traces of human settlement in Arabia from at least 40,000 years ago. Massive and widespread petroglyphs (rock art), carved in low relief on rock faces, abound in northern Saudi Arabia, the finest example at a site called Jubbah, north of Hail. These date from Neolithic settlements of 10,000 years ago.

The oceans surrounding the Arabian Peninsula provided natural transportation routes between the Tigris-Euphrates valley, the Indus valley (in today's Pakistan), and the Red Sea. Very early archeological remains have been found on islands off the eastern shore of the Arabian Peninsula and beside the natural harbors along the coasts. A network of caravan routes, controlled by the Arabs, linked these ports to the Mediterranean.

Myrrh and frankincense (fragrant gum resins from indigenous shrubs) as well as goods from India and Africa, were eagerly sought by the Mediterranean peoples for religious ceremonies and cosmetic purposes. Ships that plied the Indian Ocean unloaded their cargoes at ports in southern Arabia to be transported north by camel. Great caravans, consisting of hundreds of camels, moved across the desert wastes and through the rocky mountain valleys from waterhole to wellspring. Tent cities sprang instantly to life when they camped and vanished just as quickly as they moved on. The tribes that controlled the watering places and owned the camels prospered on the fees they received. The remains of an ancient trading center called Taima, a way station on the caravan route between Egypt and Babylon are scattered across a huge plain on the edge of the Nafud region in Saudi Arabia.

From about 350 B.C. to 100 A.D. an Arab tribe called the Nabateans controlled the northern end of the Incense Trail. They left behind massive stone-carved facades of temples and tombs, not only at Petra, their capital city located in today's Jordan, but also at several locations in northern Arabia—Madain Salah, Al Ula, Qurayyat, Al Bida, and Rawwafah. Archeologists are at work today deciphering the clues to the past hidden in these ancient ruins.

The Romans destroyed the Nabatean kingdom in the second century A.D. The indigenous tribes were eventually caught in a fierce struggle for control of the trade in Arabia, waged by the western Roman empire against the invading Persians, whose imperial power in the east had already waxed and waned for many centuries. The Persians considered the Gulf coast of the Arabian Peninsula to be part of their maritime trading complex, but Persian domination was interrupted by the career of the best-known Arab of all time.

The Prophet Muhammad Inspires the Arabs

Muhammad was a member of the Quraysh tribe, which governed Makkah, controlled its water rights, and cared for its major pilgrimage shrine, the Kaabah. Muhammad belonged to the Hashemite clan of the Quraysh tribe. Orphaned at an early age, Muhammad was raised by a well-placed uncle, who took his nephew on his commercial expeditions. Little is known of Muhammad's youth, except that he visited the leading trading centers of the region and was employed in his twenties to manage the caravans of a wealthy widow, Khadija, who had inherited a thriving commercial business. Although Muhammad was several years younger than Khadija, he married her when he was twenty-four, and led thereafter the life of a well-to-do merchant. His excellent character earned him the title *Al Amin*—the trustworthy.

THE BIRTH OF THE MUSLIM RELIGION

When he was about forty, Muhammad became very troubled by the erosion of moral values, exploitation of wealth, and extreme social inequities in Makkah. Pilgrimages to the many pagan shrines in that city attracted hordes of merchants, poets, entertainers, gamblers, prostitutes—the array that always gathers wherever travelers can be parted from their money. Repelled by this display of greed, Muhammad turned to religious study. While he was meditating in a mountain cave, he began having visions and hearing revelations telling him that God had chosen him to be the vehicle for teaching the true religion to his people. They should abandon their pagan idols and worship only *Allah*, who is the creator and provider—the one who aids men in peril. Muhammad became the prophet of that deity, whose followers today include one-fifth of the world's total population.

God's messages, transmitted to Muhammad by the Archangel Gabriel, continued throughout Muhammad's life and were later incorporated into the holy book of Islam, the *Quran* (Koran), which means "recitation."

Ye who believe! Stand out firmly for justice, as witnesses to God, even as against yourselves, or your parents, or your kin, and whether it be (against rich or poor: For God can best protect both. Follow not the lusts (of your hearts), lest ye swerve, and if ye distort (justice) or decline to do justice, verily God is well-acquainted with all that ye do.

Qur'an: IV, 135

Muhammad's doctrine, when he began preaching, was a very simple instruction that his people should abandon their many idols and worship one God. The faith revealed to him was called Islam, which means "submission." The message was parallel to that of both the Jewish and Christian faiths. Important Jewish colonies were scattered throughout the Arabian Peninsula in Muhammad's time, and Jews were active in the commercial life of the area known as Hijaz, of which Makkah was the central city and an important caravan stop. Several Christian sects had also spread along the edges of Arabia, particularly in Syria, in the Hira Mountains to the northeast of Makkah, and in Yemen. When he began spreading God's word, Muhammad considered his message a continuation of those earlier prophetic traditions.

Say: He is God, The One and Only; God, the Eternal, Absolute; He begetteth not, nor is He begotten; and there is none like unto Him.

Qur'an: CXII, 1-4

Muhammad's first converts were his wife and a cousin named Ali, who married his daughter Fatima and years later became one of his successors in leadership of the Muslim faithful. Gradually, as Muhammad expanded his message to emphasize the brotherhood and equality of all those who embraced Islam, he gathered converts from the poor and dispossessed classes of Makkah. The merchant aristocracy of the city, particularly Muhammad's own Quraysh tribe, soon became alarmed because the city thrived on the commerce connected with the worship of pagan gods and the profitable pilgrimages to their shrines. Islam's condemnation of these cults threatened Quraysh prosperity.

The Hijrah from Makkah to Madinah

After a decade of ridicule and persecution, Prophet Muhammad escaped the opposition of the Quraysh chiefs by accepting an invitation from a group in Yathrib, 250 miles to the northeast, to make that city his home. About two hundred of his followers moved quietly from Makkah to Yathrib, with Muhammad following in 622. This event, the first certain date in Muslim history, has been known to Muslims ever since as the hejira (from the Arabic *hijrah*, meaning "migration"), and serves as the starting year of the Muslim calendar. Yathrib soon became known as Al Madinah (Medina)—"the city of the Prophet."

TABLE 1
COMPARISON OF MUSLIM AND CHRISTIAN CALENDARS

Anno Hejirae 1390 began on 9 March 1970 A.D.
1400 began on 21 November 1979
1410 began on 4 August 1989
1420 begins on 17 April 1999
1421 begins on 6 April 2000

Source: Zaki M. A. Farsi, *National Guide & Atlas of the Kingdom of Saudi Arabia* (Jeddah, Saudi Arabia, 1989)

The men of Medina who had extended the invitation to Muhammad were particularly impressed by his leadership ability, for they needed someone of forceful character to mediate the clan disputes that were wracking their city. The prophet acted as governor of the small Muslim community, and considerably enhanced his position by reaching an accommodation with the large Jewish community in Madinah. The differences between Old Testament scripture and Muhammad's Quran soon made the Jews scornful, however, and he turned away from them when they would not accept the fact that his revelation came directly from God.

The prophet emphasized a pre-Hebrew source for his message—that Abraham (the Old Testament prophet) was the patriarch of Islam. The ancestry of the Quraysh, who ruled Makkah, was traced to Abraham's first son Ishmail, while the Hebrews were descended from his second son Isaac. Abraham had begun the pilgrimage to Makkah and erected the Kaabah there. The Prophet Muhammad sought to purify Makkah of all the pagan idols that had been added since the time of Abraham. He established the day of prayer to Friday, appointed a professional "crier" (*muezzin*) to call the faithful to prayer, and decreed a month of fasting (Ramadan) and an annual pilgrimage as Pillars of the Muslim faith.

The prophet quickly gained converts from many of the Arabian tribes, but he needed more than authority for his community to thrive. He proved to be not only a prophet, but an astute military strategist. Economic resources for his people were secured from rich caravans moving to and from Makkah,—retribution imposed on the corrupt and ungodly merchants.

The Return to Makkah

The merchants of Makkah fought several futile battles against the Muslims. Finally in 628 they negotiated a ten-year truce which gave the Muslims the right to make their annual pilgrimage to the Kaabah. In 630, however, the murder of a Muslim pilgrim provided an excuse to break the truce, and Makkah was invaded and occupied. The Prophet immediately destroyed all the relics in Makkah except for the large black meteorite which was housed in the Kaabah.

Then Muhammad openly declared the new religion. He decreed that the faithful would henceforth pray toward Makkah rather than Jerusalem, and that the Kaabah in Makkah was the center of the new faith and the focus of its pilgrimage. Nevertheless, all the revealed books—the Torah, the Psalms, the Gospel, and the Quran remained sacred. Those who believe in revealed scripture were called "people of the book"—*Ahl al Kitab.*

The Prophet died in 632—after a 23-year period of revelation— at the peak of his career. He was then triumphant in the city of his birth and recognized as the head of a powerful and growing community, tied together by monotheism and focused through a revealed scripture. The fragmented Arabian tribes had needed a simple doctrine that could unify them and replace the multiple rivalries and religious idolatries that had divided the clans one from another. The earlier monotheistic faiths, Judaism and Christianity, which had been spreading around the fringes of the Arabian Peninsula, had complex codes—more suited to settled people—and did not sit comfortably with the fiercely independent Bedouin.

Islam offered a simple ethical ideal in the form of a commandment from God that required no great break with Bedouin customs. It involved no intricate theology, no priesthood, no rigid hierarchy, no allegiance except to God. Every man who abandoned the idolatry and fierce rivalry that prevailed in those days could become holy, and any man could be an *imam*—a leader of prayers. All that was required was a profession of belief in the one true God.

> Establish regular prayer, enjoin what is just, and forbid what is wrong; and bear with patient constancy whate'er betide thee; for this is firmness (of purpose) in (the conduct of) affairs. And swell not thy cheek (for pride) at men, nor walk in insolence through the earth; for God loveth not any arrogant boaster. And be moderate in thy pace, and lower thy voice; for the harshest of sounds without doubt is the braying of the ass.
>
> *Qur'an: XXXI, 17-19*

The Outward Thrust of Islam

Within a century after their Prophet's death, the Muslims had spilled out of the Arabian Peninsula to forge an empire which stretched from the Atlantic to the Indus River. Nothing about this expansion of their realm was planned. The Bedouin of the desert were warriors by birth and training, learning at an early age to defend their water and pasturage. Islam taught them an ideology that stressed equality and justice. Buoyed by the vitality of their new faith, they swept into the provinces of the two oppressive empires to the north—Sassanian Iran and Christian Byzantium.

The Muslim expansion began immediately after Muhammad's death. No sons survived him, nor had he made any provision for succession to his position as head of the Muslim community. The Muslim community elected Abu Bakr, as his successor (*khalifa*—caliph). But some of the other Arabian tribes who had embraced the faith regarded their allegiance as personal to the Prophet. When he died, they considered that chapter closed and went their separate ways. Abu Bakr announced to the faithful: "Those who worship Muhammad should know Muhammad has died; those who worship God know God is eternal." So he set in motion a military campaign that quickly established control over most of the Arabian Peninsula.

United under one banner, the Muslims spilled across their own borders, using their horse and camel cavalry, which were instantly mobile and proved devastating in open country. The border tribes were far too disorganized to resist this united onslaught. Nor were they eager to fight for the Persian and Byzantine despots who controlled them.

Communications were too slow for military conquest to be directed by the caliph in Medina. Each time his military commanders in the field met with success, they made simple on-the-spot decisions as to where to launch their next thrust. Often local inhabitants suggested the next move, and joined the Muslims against their oppressive rulers. These lightning strikes created chaos among the cumbersome phalanxes of the Persians and the Byzantines.

These spontaneous campaigns brought rich rewards in booty and tribute to the warriors, and spurred enthusiasm for the Muslim faith. Islam provided the rallying cry and the unifying force that sparked a series of remarkable political and military successes.

The Rapid Spread of Islam

Abu Bakr died in 634; his successor Caliph Umar (Omar) was as close to the prophet as Abu Bakr. He instructed his followers to preserve Muhammad's revelations by writing them down in a holy book that became the Quran. (The authoritative version of the Quran was recorded in 651 A.D.) Then he set about systematically organizing a civil administration and consolidating the Muslim empire.

Umar carried his campaigns first into Syria, entering its most important city, Damascus, in 635. The army Byzantium sent against him in 636 was routed, opening Syria completely to Muslim rule. What is today called Iraq was taken in 637, Jerusalem in 638, giving the Muslims control of the Fertile Crescent, that rich farming area that stretches from the Nile Valley across the Middle East to the Tigris-Euphrates Valley. The Muslims swept eastward, across Persia, through what is today Afghanistan, and by 643 reached the Indus River in what is now Pakistan.

If the coastline of Syria was to be held, the Muslims had to control Egypt, which was a major maritime province of Byzantium, ruled from Constantinople. In 640 Alexandria, the Egyptian capital founded nine hundred years earlier by Alexander the Great, was besieged and taken. In Egypt too the local population welcomed the Muslims as a relief from the tyranny of their Byzantine rulers. When they were given the choice between paying a tax for Muslim protection or joining the brotherhood of Islam, most of these neighboring peoples chose Islam. Subject peoples soon recognized the material benefits of converting to Islam, and through the long process of Islamic expansion, growing numbers of local people chose to learn Arabic, adopt Arab customs, and embrace the faith. Eventually the subjects outnumbered their Arab rulers and overshadowed them. The egalitarian principles of Islam soon dissolved the distinctions between the two groups, and both became part of a single Muslim community.

The Schism Between the Sunnis and the Shiites

The unity of the new Muslim society was disrupted by disagreements when it came to naming a new caliph. Abu Bakr and Umar had been close companions of the prophet and were also from the Hashemite clan. When Umar died, the rival Umayyad clan of the same Quraysh tribe of Makkah succeeded in putting one of their members, Uthman (Othman), who had been a close associate of the Prophet, into the caliphate. Uthman was murdered in 656.

This event led to a rupture among Muslims that has never been mended—between those who believe that the caliph, as the Prophet's successor, should be of hereditary descent from Muhammad's inner circle of companions, and those who maintain that the protector of the Muslim faith should be chosen by consensus from the Quraysh tribe.

The closest remaining member of the Prophet's inner circle was Ali, husband of Muhammad's daughter Fatima, but the Umayyad clan refused to accept his election as caliph. Ali led an army across the Tigris-Euphrates plains and moved his headquarters from Madinah to Kufa (in what is now southern Iraq). Supporters of the Umayyads soon plotted against Ali. With the help of chiefs in Egypt, the governor of Syria forced Ali to negotiate. The next four years saw bitter factionalism. Finally in 660 the Umayyads chose the Syrian governor, Muawiyah, to be their leader. Ali was assassinated a year and a half later.

The first four caliphs had been close associates of Muhammad. Muawiyah was not a Makkan; Syria was his home and he immediately moved the caliphate to Damascus. He skillfully developed an effective organization for administering his realm and a disciplined army, which continued to push eastward and westward along the lines of least resistance. He chose his son as his successor and thus established the principal of hereditary succession.

When Muawiyah died, however, Ali's supporters (known by now as Shia or Shiites) began agitating again to shift the caliphate back to Iraq and replace Muawiyah's successor with Ali's second son Husayn (the Prophet's grandson). The Shiites maintained that only descendants of Ali, their first *imam*, could truly lead the faithful and interpret the Quran. Husayn was killed in the battle of Karbala (in what is now southern Iraq) in 680. His martyrdom provided a focal point for the schism that has persisted between Shiites and Sunnis ever since.

The battling among the clans over the next sixty years destroyed the unity of Muslim leadership. The Arabians split into warring factions, and their obsession with the quarrel gave rise to the distinction between northern and southern Arabs that persists today. The internal struggle was matched by a schism between the Persians, who had supported Ali, and most of the Arabs who supported the Umayyads against those allied with the great clans of Madinah.

This schism still persists in the two great branches of Islam known as Shia and Sunni. The Sunni, who are far more numerous, take their name from the *sunnah*—the words and traditions of the Prophet. They regarded the caliph as only the secular head of state, whereas the Shia regarded their imam as both spiritual and secular ruler. Shiite Muslims predominate today in Iran, Iraq, Bahrain, and Yemen, and are present in sizable numbers in the Eastern Province of Saudi Arabia.

An Arab Empire Outside of Arabia

By the middle of the eighth century the Damascus caliphate was no longer recognized outside Syria, and the caliph of this time was the last of the Umayyads. In 747 a revolt against the Umayyads was spearheaded by their cousins, the Abbas clan, then living in Persia. The Arabian tribes were too disunited to resist. Umayyad power disintegrated; Umayyad family members were massacred in Damascus by the Abbas family; and the Abbasids appointed a caliph. This was, in effect, the end of Arabian control of the Muslim empire, for Arabian blood was by now so mixed with that of other peoples that a new society had emerged. The Arabian aristocracy was no longer necessary to the maintenance of the empire. For the next five hundred years the Abbasid caliphs ruled the eastern empire from Baghdad, a new city of their own creation, permeated by Persian culture.

The Muslim empire expanded westward as well. The fall of Egypt had left the Byzantine provinces of North Africa open to invasion. The Arabs succeeded over a period of several decades and after many reverses in subjugating the Berbers of North Africa, and the Berbers in turn joined the forward rush of Islam. Berber soldiers were essential in carrying the faith to the Atlantic coast and in the armies that crossed from Morocco to conquer and rule Spain.

Gothic rule in the Spains had been tyrannical, earning universal hatred, and internal strife permitted the Spanish cities to fall easily to the Muslims. A Muslim province called Andalusia (*al Andalus*) was swiftly established in the conquered territories. The northward movement of the Muslim armies into Europe was finally halted in France exactly a century after the Prophet's death, when Arab-Berber forces were defeated in 732 in a battle between Poitiers and Tours. Christian Europe viewed this alien force ensconced on its perimeter as the arch enemy of Western civilization, an attitude that prevailed for centuries.

Spain remained under Muslim control for three hundred years. An illustrious branch of the Umayyad family ruled in Cordova from 929 to 1031—a period of unusual religious tolerance, which ended in 1492 when the last Muslim state fell to Spanish reconquest.

In the east, the further expansion of Islam after the 8th century was peaceful, carried out over a long period of time by itinerant traders. They carried the faith to the East Indies and south across the Sahara to black Africa. Muslim government was generally very tolerant of non-Muslims. The particularly benevolent rule of the Abbasids greatly encouraged wholesale mass conversions. Most of later Muslim mission work was carried on peacefully, by converts rather than by the Arabs.

ISLAMIC ART

Muslim art "found its highest expression in calligraphy and ornaments. The arabesque, that is, strictly speaking, a tendril that grows through leaves, palmettes, and flowers without end, ever expanding, is the central motif of Islamic art. The decorative pattern of the—seemingly—central motif continues infinitely by being doubled, halved, or by means of simple or twisted mirror effects, all based on sophisticated mathematical rules. Thus the design draws the eye upward and makes the meditating spirit remember the infinite and inexhaustible power of God. Along with calligraphy (which again is transformed into ornament) and which translates and announces God's word, the arabesque is a suitable ornament for both the Sacred Book and the sacred space."

Annemarie Schimmel, *Islam* (Albany: State University of New York Press, 1992)

ARAB LEARNING AND CULTURE

Within a century after the establishment of Baghdad, the Arabs had translated the chief philosophical works of Aristotle, of the leading Neo-Platonic commentators, the *Elements* of Euclid, the *Almagest* of Ptolemy, and most of the medical writings of Hippocrates and Galen (his seven books on anatomy were lost in the original Greek and survived only in Arabic). Through Arab scholars, particularly Avicenna (Ibn Sina) and Averroes, these works eventually found their way into Latin to become a determining influence upon medieval European scholasticism.

The Abbasids delved as well into much of Persian and Indian scientific writing. Al Khawarizmi's widely known astronomical tables were one result; he also wrote the first book on algebra. Important educational institutions were established—combinations of library, academy, and translation bureau. A paper mill was erected in Baghdad after the manufacture of writing paper was introduced from China in 751. Optics and geometry are part of Islamic heritage.

Muhammad ibn Zakariyya al Razi was the first to identify and treat smallpox, to use alcohol as an antiseptic, and to make medical use of mercury as a purgative. Ibn Sina identified and treated meningitis and wrote a masterpiece that was the final authority in medicine for six centuries.

Muslim contributions to mathematics had perhaps the greatest direct influence on our lives today. Al Biruni established trigonometry as a distinct branch of mathematics, while other Muslim scholars developed the theory of numbers. Sometime before 800 A.D. the Arabs adopted the Indian system of using smaller clusters of written number symbols than the Latin, thus greatly simplifying written computations. The numerals themselves are probably based on the Arabic alphabet, and the Arabs introduced the concept of zero to indicate a unitary value of nothing. (The Arabic *sifr*, cipher in English, means "empty.") Their numerals were carried to Spain about 900, and transmitted thus to the rest of Europe after 1100. The ten basic symbols—0 through 9—in which all numbers can be expressed were so much simpler than any others in use that Arabic numerals became the most commonly used throughout the world.

The Legacy of the Muslim Empire

The Abbasid caliphate proved to be the Golden Age of Islam, which was a legacy begun by the Muslims of Arabia, but not their creation. They had spilled out of the Arabian desert and been absorbed by the Muslims they had converted. The use of the Arabic language reached its zenith, but power was shared by all believers.

The amalgamation of the brotherhood of Islam and the various cultures that were blended into the Muslim Empire produced an age of science, literature, art, and architecture never surpassed. The period was one of enormous prosperity based on industry, agriculture, and farflung trade: in ships that sailed to East Africa, India, the East Indies, and China; by camel caravan across the Sahara to West Africa; and along the seas and rivers of Russia. But, spectacular as was the rise of the highly civilized Muslim Empire, so was its decline swift. By the middle of the 10th century, decadence, internecine rivalry, and intrigue had fragmented the realm to the point that the caliphate soon fell to pieces.

The center of the Empire had been moved from Medina to Damascus to facilitate administration of the growing realm, and then to Baghdad as Persian influence grew predominant. While Baghdad was reaching heights of wealth, intellect, and fame as a great center of culture, Arabia itself lapsed back into stagnation. The nomadic tribes reverted to rivalry and raiding, and remained politically fragmented for nearly a thousand years.

Invaders Provoke Centuries of Decline

A Mongol onslaught which began in central Asia in 1220 replaced the Abbasid empire with new centers of authority in Iran, Turkey, and Egypt. In 1258 the Mongols invaded and destroyed Baghdad, brutally terminating the flourishing Islamic empire.

In the 15th century Europe opened up sea routes to Asia around Africa, bypassing the Middle East and severing the important overland trade links between Europe and the East that had provided so much wealth to Middle Eastern merchants. When the Ottoman Turks conquered Egypt in 1517, they carried with them to Constantinople the last of the Abbasid line in order to establish the caliphate there. The Sultan of Turkey eventually assumed the caliphal title and privileges.

TABLE 2
MAJOR DATES OF ISLAMIC HISTORY

570 A.D.	Birth of the Prophet Muhammad.
609	First verses of the Quran revealed.
622	Prophet's migration from Makkah to Medina (hijrah); the beginning of the Islamic calendar.
632	Death of the Prophet.
632-661	The "rightly guided" caliphs—Abu Bakr, Umar, Uthman, and Ali.
657	Battle of Siffin began the cleavage of Islam into Sunni and Shia branches.
661-750	Umayyads rule in Damascus.
750-1258	Abbasids rule in Baghdad.
756-1031	Umayyads rule Spain.
909-1171	Fatimids rule in Cairo.
1037-1300	Seljuqs rule Anatolia.
1171-1371	Ayyubids rule Egypt.
1187	The Ayyubid leader, Saladin, conquers Jerusalem.
1252-1517	Mamluks rule Egypt and Syria.
1258	Mongols conquer Baghdad.
1299-1924	Ottomans rule in Constantinople.
1369-1500	Timurids rule in Samarqand.
1453	Turkish conquest of Constantinople (Byzantium).
1492	Fall of Granada in Spain (last Muslim dynasty).
1501-1736	Safavids rule in Persia.
1526-1857	Moguls rule in India.

Source: Adapted from *Islam: A Global Civilization*, prepared by the Islamic Affairs Department, The Embassy of Saudi Arabia, Washington, DC.

He rapidly took control of most of the Muslim Empire, including western Arabia, and even extended Islam into the Balkans. With the end of the international trade that had provided centuries of continuous wealth to the Arabs came a long period of commercial and intellectual stagnation. Because the Ottoman Turks were absorbed in wars with Austria, Russia, and Persia, the people of the Arabian Peninsula were left in their backwater to fend for themselves.

Europe Intrudes

At about the time that the Ottoman Turks took over control of the Muslim Empire, Europeans arrived in the Gulf. The Portuguese came first, in 1507, and changed the whole pattern of trade and power in the East. In 1515 they took control of the region called Muscat and Oman on the southeastern coast of the Peninsula, and remained until 1650 in spite of periodic revolts and conflicts with the local tribes.

Other European powers were entering the competition. The English defeated Portuguese fleets in 1610, 1615, and 1620, and helped the Persians eject the Portuguese from the island of Hormuz in 1622. Between 1630 and 1650 the Imams of Oman took advantage of conflicts between the Portuguese and the Dutch to attack and seize all their ports in the Gulf. The Omanis developed great maritime skill, ranging the coasts of India and extending their control to the Portuguese settlements of East Africa.

Piracy soon became the dominant activity in the Gulf. By 1700 Muscat with its excellent natural anchorage had become a virtually independent city- state, thriving on plunder and customs duties forcibly levied on Gulf trade. Its bazaars were crowded with Socotra aloes, asafeotida, frankincense, putchok, and myrrh; minerals such as alum and sulphur; ivory from East Africa; fabrics and carpets from India; pearls from the Gulf; coffee from Mocha in Yemen. Horses, livestock, fish, dates, fruits, vegetables, and cereals were exported.

Meanwhile in the interior of the Arabian Peninsula the tribes continued their age-old struggle for power. In about 1710 several clans of the tribe called Anaza moved from the interior Najd region of Arabia to escape drought and famine, and settled in Kuwait, a small fishing village on the coast. These settlers were Sunni Muslims, cousins of the Al Saud family which would later unite Saudi Arabia. By the end of the century the Al Sabah clan of that tribe had established control of a small kingdom called Kuwait. The Ottoman Turks recognized Al Sabah authority in 1756.

In 1766 the Al Khalifa family of the same tribe migrated south from Kuwait and settled at Zubarah on the coast of the Qatar Peninsula. This town was the center of their thriving pearl trade until 1782, when the Al Khalifa attacked Bahrain and established a dynasty there which still governs the Bahrain Archipelago. This same family continued to control Qatar until it was occupied by the Turks in 1872, but they gradually moved from Qatar to Bahrain in the face of attacks by militant Muslims from interior Arabia.

Piracy in the Gulf region was still a problem in the 19th century. Great Britain intervened, ostensibly to protect trade. A campaign launched against the pirate strongholds between 1805 and 1818 ended with a General Treaty of Peace in 1820 between Britain and the shaykhs of Bahrain, Qatar, and the several fragmented shaykhdoms south of Qatar. This treaty, which guaranteed British protection and excluded other foreign powers from the area, was supplemented in 1853 by a maritime truce, enforced by Britain, and it was at that time that the shaykhdoms south of Qatar became known as the Trucial Coast.

In 1839 Britain had captured the small fishing port of Aden, located on the southwestern tip of the Peninsula. Because of its strategic location, it grew into an important trading center and coal bunkering station, particularly after the opening of the Suez Canal in 1869. Because of its commanding location at the entrance to the Indian Ocean on the route from Europe through the Mediterranean to the Orient, Aden became a thriving commercial city long before World War II.

To protect their vital interest in Aden, the British soon found it necessary to extend their control eastward and to develop treaty relationships with the many independent shaykhs of the hinterland. Sixteen shaykhdoms which accepted British protection became the Western Protectorate and four were included in the Eastern Protectorate—forerunners of today's Yemen.

The Bedouin Rally to New Banners

While Britain was extending its influence along the Arabian coasts, a major reform movement was under way in the interior. In the early 1700s a Muslim religious leader from central Arabia was fired with a zeal to return his people to the strict and simple message of the Quran and the teachings of the Prophet Muhammad. Shaykh Muhammad ibn Abd al Wahhab had received a deeply religious education, and was determined to cleanse Islam of the festivals, pageantry, superstitions, mysticism, and saint-worship that had been added to it over the years.

He and his followers saw their Ottoman rulers practicing that same idolatry—using opulent, exotic art forms in their mosques, building splendid monuments to their leaders, revering tombs of Sufi saints, and indulging in ecstatic experiences. Frightened by Shaykh Muhammad's fierce harangues, the local residents drove him from his home town. He found refuge in Dariyah, not far from Riyadh, where the governing Al Saud family welcomed and supported him.

Shaykh Muhammad's followers were generally known as Wahhabis, and it was under the banners of this strict religious sect that the Al Saud family conquered the tribes of central and western Arabia in the late 1700s and early 1800s. The Ottoman Turks countered by sending their allies, the Egyptians, to defeat the Wahhabis in 1816. Although the Bedouin had become nominal Muslims in the Prophet's time, they had refused to change their tribal way of life. Raiding, blood feuds, and vengeance continued to be their principal preoccupation until the 20th century, when Abdul Aziz ibn Saud gathered them under his control, imposed law and order throughout his realm, and created the nation known as the Kingdom of Saudi Arabia.

Even today the faith practiced in Saudi Arabia and the Gulf shaykhdoms is much stricter than in other parts of the Muslim world. Saudi Arabia's association with the life of the Prophet and the presence of the holy cities of Makkah and Medina within its borders make Islam a primary force in shaping life and society. The Saudis who regard themselves as *Salafi*—descendants of that first generation of devout Muslims who surrounded the Prophet—are the puritans of Islam. Muslim law (*al sharia*) is the basis of government; the prohibitions of the Quran and *hadith* (sayings of the Prophet) are strictly observed; and social relationships are truly egalitarian. No non-Muslim ruler has ever, since Muhammad's time, controlled any of Saudi Arabia. No non-Muslim has visited the holy shrines except in disguise. Citizenship requires a declaration of the faith. Immigrants can convert to Islam, but Muslims do not repudiate their religion. They are particularly intolerant of agnosticism or atheism, for they find indifference to religion incomprehensible.

ISLAM AS A WAY OF LIFE

Islamic religious law (sharia) governs society in Saudi Arabia; the government's function is to enforce the sharia. Consequently, the outlook and ethics of the Saudis are very much determined by the tenets of their faith.

Islam means "submission to, or having peace with God." Those who submit are called Muslims. Although the Prophet of Islam was Muhammad, Muslims dislike being called Muhammadans because that implies that they worship Muhammad or that Muhammad invented their faith. They worship only God, whom they call Allah (al ilah, meaning "the Supreme Being" in Arabic, as well as in Aramaic, the language of Jesus), and they believe that Islam is the last message of God revealed to his messenger, the Prophet Muhammad.

Muhammad never claimed to have supernatural powers or to be anything more than an ordinary human being. He regarded himself simply as a man whom God had chosen to receive a perfected revelation of His will, which Muhammad clarified and directed to his people. No biography of Muhammad was written until 140 years after his death, for his close followers regarded his message as far more important than the details of his life. Nevertheless, later generations of Muslims ornamented his memory with a mantle of legend and mysticism far beyond anything he or his companions ever intended.

The bulk of Muslim theology is concerned with Allah. He has ninety-nine names and as many attributes, and many devout Muslim repeat Allah's name following prayers five times a day. (The use of beads (*subhah*) in prayer to help recall the ninety-nine names of God was a custom of Indian origin, adopted by a Sufi sect of Islam in about the 9th century. Mainstream Sunni Muslims do not use "worry beads." Catholics started using the rosary in the 13th century, after the Crusaders had seen the Sufi custom.)

The most beautiful names belong to God: So call on Him by them; but shun such men as use profanity in His names: For what they do, they will soon be requited.

Qur'an: VII, 180

The Five Pillars of Islam

The basic tenets of Islam are five in number, and are known as the Pillars of the Faith. The first is the profession of faith (*shahadah*), which is all that is required to become a convert: *Ash'hadu ann la ilaha illa'Llah: wa anna Muhammadan rasulu 'Llah."* I hereby bear witness that there is no God but Allah: and that Muhammad is His messenger." These words are probably repeated more often than any other single phrase on earth.

The second pillar is prayer (salat): the faithful are called to pray five times a day. At dawn, at mid- day, at mid-afternoon, at sunset, and nightfall all good Muslims respond to the call of the muezzin, turn their faces toward Makkah, and recite their prayers, following prescribed movements which emphasize humility and devotion and also happen to be good exercise. The hours of prayer vary with the seasons and are published in the newspapers. All business, commercial, and government activity stops in Saudi Arabia during prayers.

THE CALL TO PRAYER

God is most great. God is most great.
God is most great. God is most great.
I testify that there is no god except God.
I testify that there is no god except God.
I testify that Muhammad is the messenger of God.
I testify that Muhammad is the messenger of God.
Come to prayer! Come to prayer!
Come to success (in this life and the Hereafter)!
Come to success!
God is most great. God is most great.
There is no god except God.

The third pillar of Islam is almsgiving (zakat), which originally was intended to support the poor and needy among the Muslim community, to build mosques, and to defray administrative expenses. In some Muslim countries it is now left to one's conscience; in others it is collected as a tax. Saudi Arabia has a Department of Zakat within the Ministry of Finance, which distributes the contributions of Saudi citizens (up to 2.5 percent of an individual's resources beyond his immediate needs) to those less fortunate. (There are no income taxes in the kingdom.)

The fourth pillar is fasting (sawm), a custom which was well established at the time of revelation among both Christians and Jews. It is an exercise of self-control through which one's sensitivity is heightened to the glory of God and the sufferings of the poor. Islam prescribed the month of Ramadan (the ninth month of the lunar calendar) as a time of total abstinence from food, drink, smoking, and sexual relations during the daylight hours. Since the Muslim calendar is based on the lunar cycle, Ramadan occurs at different times throughout the year. When it falls during hot summer months, fasting in Saudi Arabia is an act of real suffering and privation, and makes the Muslim very aware of those in want. Work days are cut to six hours to make the fast more bearable.

> O ye who believe! Fasting is prescribed for you as it was prescribed to those before you, that ye may (learn) self-restraint.
>
> *Qur'an: II, 183*

The fifth pillar of Islam is pilgrimage (hajj), an ancient Arab tradition which Muhammad focused on the pilgrimage of Abraham to Makkah. Every Muslim, if he or she is able, must go once to the holy shrines in Makkah and Medina between the eighth and thirteenth days of the last month (*Dhu al Hijrah*) of the Islamic calendar. Air travel, introduced in the 1950s, has greatly simplified and shortened the time involved.

Men wear a seamless garment identical to those of all other pilgrims, women a covering garment, and the multitude performs prescribed rites that renew their ties to the origins of their faith. Over the centuries since the Prophet's time, the pilgrimage has been one of the major unifying forces in Islam, the common bond that ties diverse believers from countries all over the globe into a single community of believers (ummah). The Saudi government values this opportunity to extend hospitality to Muslims worldwide, from heads of state to the most ordinary peasant.

Customs Deriving from Islam

Islam has much in common with Judaism and Christianity. Islam asserts Jewish revelations in the Torah (the first five books of the Old Testament), except for the covenant between God and the Hebrews and the special status of a Chosen People; and Christian revelations in the Gospels, excluding the divinity of Jesus and the concept of the Trinity. Islam regards Jesus as one in a long line of God's prophets, beginning with Adam, moving through Abraham and Moses, including Jesus, and ending with Muhammad as the final voice for God's divine revelation and the Quran as the perfected vehicle for its transmission.

TABLE 3
PILGRIMS ARRIVING IN MAKKAH
(not including Saudi citizens)

1402	(1982)	853,555
1403	(1983)	1,003,911
1404	(1984)	919,671
1405	(1985)	851,761
1406	(1986)	856,718
1407	(1987)	960,386
1409	(1989)	774,560
1410	(1990)	827,236
1411	(1991)	720,102

Source: Ministry of Finance and National Economy, *Statistical Yearbook,* Kingdom of Saudi Arabia, 1991

Say ye: "We believe in God, and the revelation given to us, and to Abraham, Ishmail, Isaac, Jacob, and the tribes, and that given to Moses and Jesus, and that given to (all) Prophets from their Lord: We make no difference between one and another of them: and we bow to God (in Islam).
Qur'an: II, 136

Many of the Quran's instructions were aimed at ameliorating the social injustices on earth. Slavery was permitted under certain conditions, although the Quran urged that slaves be freed. Faith, patience,

kindness, honesty, industry, honor, courage, and generosity were emphasized as desirable virtues. Other beliefs included a general resur-
rection, a final judgment of all mankind by God, eternal life in the
hereafter, and God's knowledge of every man's acts and ultimate fate.
The philosophical basis in Islam for striving to achieve heavenly rewards
is not identical to the Christian. Where Jesus promised heaven as a
reward for being and doing good, Islam promises paradise to those
who are righteous, who surrender to the might and majesty of God.

God will admit those who believe and work righteous deeds to Gardens
beneath which rivers flow: they shall be adorned therein with bracelets
of gold and pearls; and their garments there will be of silk. For they have
been guided (in this life) to the purest of speeches; they have been guided
to the Path of Him who is Worthy of (all) Praise.

Qur'an: XXII, 23-24

Islam presented a new religious law, which was to regulate not
only legal decisions, but also basic beliefs, religious practices, and social
behavior. This law was to put an end to the incessant conflict between
the tribes and their preoccupation with genealogical status by
eliminating all previous distinctions so that individuals would be judged
only by the degree of their faith. Because Islamic law is religious, its
study becomes a form of worship, and the person who knows and
understands the Quran and sharia automatically possesses decisive
authority and prestige.

In the two centuries after the Prophet's death, four theological
schools of jurisprudence were developed among the Sunni Muslims—
the Hanbali, the Shafi, the Hanafi, and the Maliki—each named after
its founder. Each school attempted to interpret and apply the spirit
and meaning of the Quran and sunnah (the sayings and traditions of
the Prophet) in making judgments about emerging problems in its community. Judges derive their legal judgments from these various schools.
The Hanbali school, followed in Saudi Arabia, is the most orthodox
in keeping with traditional interpretations.

The social organization of the area known today as Saudi Arabia
was, before the advent of Islam, starkly simple and nomadic. No domi-

nant outside civilizations imposed elements of their culture as happened in other Muslim countries. In the 18th century this long unbroken tradition was vitalized by a dynamic crusade inspired by Muhammad ibn Abd al Wahhab. His goal was to purify Islam in Arabia through austerity, discipline, and return to the principles practiced by the Prophet. As a result, Islam pervades both social and political life in Saudi Arabia with an intensity unique among Muslim nations.

Custodian of the Holy Shrines of Islam

Saudi kings take great pride in being custodians of the holy Muslim sanctuaries in Makkah and Medina. Every annual Saudi budget contains generous funds for the maintenance and expansion of the holy sites and the accommodation of pilgrims. The Holy Mosque in Makkah will eventually accommodate over a million worshippers, while the capacity of the Prophet's Mosque in Medina is being increased from 280,000 to 455,000 worshippers. In addition, airports, roads, transportation, lodging, fresh water, food, sanitation, and health care facilities are all provided so that the pilgrims make their hajj in comfort and safety.

Muslims everywhere hold Saudi Arabia in special esteem. There are close to a billion Muslims around the world today, and the numbers are growing, probably because of the universal appeal of the principle of brotherhood and equality of all human beings in the eyes of God. The largest Muslim communities are in the Middle East, North Africa, Afghanistan, Pakistan, India, Bangladesh, Malaysia, and Indonesia. Muslim minorities live in all the countries of Africa bordering the southern edge of the Sahara, on the east coast of Africa, in the southern Philippines, in Central Asia, in China, and in Europe in Turkey, Albania, and Yugoslavia.

Between six and eight million Muslims live today in the United States—immigrants, children of immigrants, and a steadily growing number of converts, particularly among the African-American community.

*King Saud
Bin Abdul Aziz
ruled 1953-1964*

*King Faisal
Bin Abdul Aziz
ruled 1964-1975*

*King Khalid
Bin Abdul Aziz
ruled 1975-1982*

*Custodian of the Two Holy Mosques
King Fahd Bin Abdul Aziz Al-Saud*

For over 1,400 years, the Qur'an has illuminated the lives of Muslims with its eloquent message.

Expansion work on the Holy Mosque (above) and the Prophet's Mosque in Madinah (below) has more than doubled the size of Islam's two holiest sites.

Chapter 3
THE MODERN KINGDOM

Saudi Arabia is the only major nation whose constitution is sacred scripture, the Holy Quran. Its political system is not based on that of any colonial power, but rather was devised by King Abdul Aziz Ibn Saud as he united the tribes of the Arabian Peninsula under his rule during the 1920s and 1930s. His governing principles derived almost exclusively from his determination to govern according to the purest principles of Islam and tribal traditions.

Shall we treat those who believe and work deeds of righteousness the same as those who do mischief on earth? Shall we treat those who guard against evil the same as those who turn aside from the right?

Qur'an: XXXVIII, 28

RISE OF THE SAUDI STATE

The history of modern Saudi Arabia began in the middle of the 18th century with an alliance between Muhammad bin Saud, a leader from a small town called Dariyah in the Najd region of central Arabia, and Muhammad bin Abd al Wahhab, a fervent religious scholar who sought to cleanse and reform his society by a return to a literal application of the Quran and Sunnah.

Expelled from his own community by elements who disliked his puritanical message, Muhammad bin Abd al Wahhab found refuge in Dariyah, where the Al Saud family was fired by his call to purify Islam of the mysticism and saint worship that had been added to it over the centuries. The combined forces of the two groups captured most of Najd, the central plateau of the Arabian Peninsula, before Muhammad bin Saud's death in 1765, and the alliance was strengthened by the marriage of Bin Saud's eldest son to a daughter of Abd al Wahhab.

Early in the 19th century the House of Saud took control of the Islamic holy cities of Makkah (Mecca) and Medina in western Arabia, along with parts of what are today Syria and Iraq. In 1815 the Ottoman Turks, whose nominal territory had been broached, ordered their viceroy in Egypt to recapture their Arabian domain and expel the Al Sauds from Dariyah. Later, as the Ottoman empire deteriorated, rivalries between competing clans plunged the Arabian Peninsula into a century of political conflict and confusion.

Ibn Saud's Capture of Riyadh in 1902

A grandson of the fifth generation removed from Muhammad bin Saud led his family back to Najd. Abd al Aziz bin Abd al Rahman al Saud, known in the West as Abdul Aziz Ibn Saud, left Kuwait with a small group of men and captured Riyadh by stealth in 1902. He then proceeded to forge alliances with the other Bedouin tribes of Arabia through his zeal for strict adherence to Islam, as well as by a series of astute marriages— both his own and those of other close male relatives— to daughters of chiefs of all the leading tribes. Al Saud men also married the widows and adopted the children of important allies and enemies killed in battle, forging strong ties with both friend and foe. Abdul Aziz drove the Ottoman Turks out of Hofuf in Eastern Arabia in 1913.

Devout Bedouin had between 1912 and 1917 formed a religious brotherhood known as the Ikhwan, which— spurred by enthusiasm for bringing the nomadic tribes back to the true faith—rallied to Abdul Aziz. They suited his needs perfectly. He gave them land to start 200 settlements, which formed a foundation of 60,000 fighting men. In the following two decades they rode under his banners to defeat the powerful Rashid tribe in Hail in 1921, and to replace the Hashemite rulers of the Hijaz (who had traditionally controlled the holy cities) in Makkah and Medina in 1924. Great Britain, by then the major imperial power in the Gulf area, withdrew the support given to the Hashemites during World War I, and eventually recognized Abdul Aziz instead.

British control of Transjordan, Iraq, Kuwait, and the Trucial Coast after World War I determined Abdul Aziz's northern and eastern borders. With the imposition of law and order under his leadership, the Ikhwan had no enemies left to raid or conquer, and became increasingly fractious. Unsanctioned forays across the northern borders—the last outburst of the Bedouin chiefs who had followed Abdul Aziz in holy war and helped him forge a kingdom—provoked the British. Abdul Aziz quickly allied himself with powerful families from the towns and raised an army to put down the Ikhwan revolt in 1929. This was the last military challenge to his rule.

Formation of a New Kingdom

In 1932 Abdul Aziz Ibn Saud issued a royal decree proclaiming the Kingdom of Saudi Arabia, with Riyadh as its capital and himself as king. The Saudi prefix immortalizes his ancestral line—the royal family that governs the country.

Authority in the new kingdom was focused by ideology—an exclusive identity based on Islamic faith. The new arrangement added a new focus of power in Arabia at its center. The Hijaz had previously been dominant because of its sophisticated commerce through the port of Jiddah and the worldwide Muslim pilgrimage to the holy sites of Makkah and Medina. Abdul Aziz outlined special "constitutional instructions" for the Hijaz government, named his son Faisal viceroy, and set up a consultative council of notable Hijazis to advise him. These institutions effectively consolidated the Hijaz into the Saudi kingdom.

A Central Government Under King Abdul Aziz

Under Islam, the purpose of government is to keep order, achieve justice, and protect the public interest according to Islamic law (sharia). As he consolidated his kingdom, Abdul Aziz created a highly paternalistic governing system. He and a handful of carefully chosen advisers addressed whatever problems arose. The king appointed largely autonomous amirs to administer the provinces and oversee local officials. Abdul Aziz himself distributed the revenues of the kingdom (initially very limited, derived mainly from taxes on pilgrims making the hajj; much augmented when oil revenues started flowing in the late 1940s) with the blanket generosity of the desert nomad, for whom hoarding was impossible. Ibn Saud dominated his kingdom exactly as an all-powerful patriarch would control his own extended family.

The Al Saud family was, however, much larger than usual. The network of royal progeny resulted from marriages to a number of

women from all the leading families in Arabia—including the important Wahhabis (whose descendants are known as Al Shaykh), Mutairis,
Anaizis, Dawasiris, and Sudairis. The Sudairi tie has been particularly important. King Abdul Aziz's mother was a Sudairi. Four of his
wives were of that family, accounting for 15 of his sons. Seven of them,
sons of Hassa bint Ahmad al Sudairi, are still very influential in the
kingdom. Almost thirty of Ibn Saud's sons and grandsons have married Sudairi women.

Today the royal family may number as many as 20,000 people.
An awareness of the complexity of the House of Saud—those who trace
their patrilineal ancestry directly to Muhammad bin Saud—is important, because of their dominant role in the kingdom. Untangling its
complexity is not easy, for the same names are repeated over and over,
making it necessary to trace family relationships through the ibn/bin
(son of) in every male name. Nor are all the sons of equal importance.
As in any family, the House of Saud contains members who are serious
and dedicated to the best interests of the kingdom, and others who
take no part of political affairs. The princes who matter have devoted
their careers to governing Saudi Arabia.

The main branch of the House of Saud is known as Al Faisal,
named for the paternal grandfather of Abdul Aziz. Males of this lineage,
estimated to number more than 4,000, are considered royalty and carry
the title of malaki (Royal Highness). In recent decades the key members
of the royal family have been the sons of Abdul Aziz (as many as 40
when he died, but now dwindling) and their sons of the next generation. These 200 or so male heirs of Abdul Aziz have been the key players
in Saudi affairs.

THE MODERN SAUDI GOVERNMENT

The general structure of the Saudi government is shown at Figure
1.1. It cannot be simply classified. The monarchy is not absolute (as many
Western commentators describe it), for religious law and the views of
a vast network of traditional, religious, and government leaders are
reflected in royal decisions. To rule effectively, the top echelons of the
House of Saud must be shrewd politicians rather than oriental despots.

Nor is Saudi Arabia a constitutional monarchy in the Western
sense, because the only written constitution is the Quran. But neither
is it a theocracy because in fact the king and his government run the

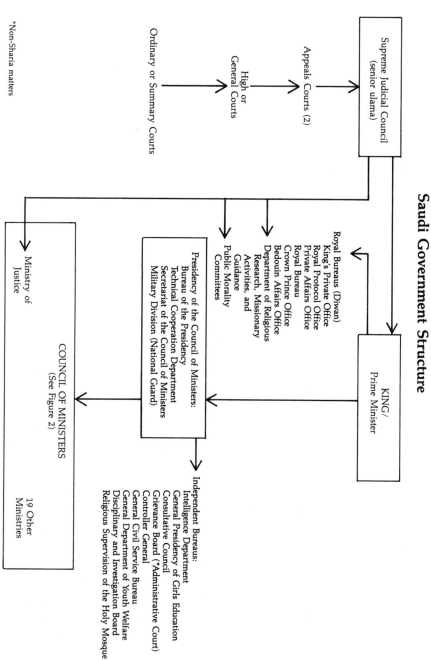

Figure 1
Saudi Government Structure

country. Perhaps Saudi Arabia could best be termed a consensus monarchy with a personalized, highly independent bureaucracy.

The religious institutions, the bureaucracy, and the military are arranged so that every power center must support the others. The kingdom has both a strong executive (the king and his government) and a strong judiciary (the Supreme Judicial Council), but no legislature and no real separation of powers in the Western sense. The name of Muslim religious law, sharia, derives from the Arabic word meaning "to legislate." According to Salafi Islamic doctrine followed in Saudi Arabia, God is the lawgiver, and no one else can legislate. Senior religious scholars have countered proposals over the years that a modern constitution be written for Saudi Arabia with the argument that God's sovereignty should not be diluted by secular legislatures. The sharia is constantly being interpreted to fit today's society, and the regular audiences held by the king and his ministers permit the expression of the people's needs and wishes.

The Monarchy

Because there is no political power structure outside the monarchy, the king's power appears absolute as long as his rule adheres to sharia. The king is prime minister, commander in chief of the armed forces, and final court of appeal. He appoints all ministers, senior government officials, governors of the provinces, ambassadors and other envoys, and military officers above the rank of lieutenant colonel. The king is assisted by the crown prince, acting as deputy prime minister and heir to the throne.

His daily affairs are conducted in the royal cabinet (*diwan*)—the primary executive office, where the king conducts most routine government affairs and holds his regular *majlis* (audience). His principal advisers for domestic politics, religious affairs, and international relations have offices there, as do the heads of several other government departments. The Department of Religious Research, Missionary Activities, and Guidance, for example, is headed by the most senior of the country's religious scholars—Shaykh Abd al Aziz bin Baz.

There seem to be no curbs on the king's powers save religious law, but in practice he is guided by traditional Muslim principles of shura (consultation) and *ijma* (consensus). These traditions obligate rulers and officials to consult with their citizens on public matters, and citizens to express their views on matters of concern to them. Final decisions should result from agreements reached by consensus.

> Help you one another in righteousness and piety, but help ye not one another in sin and rancor.
>
> *Qur'an: V, 2*

The king must also command the support of the influential members of the royal family. Who is included in the process has been the subject of endless speculation because these matters are never publicly discussed by royal insiders, and the process has varied over time. For example, 60 princes signed the 1964 resolution transferring power from King Saud to his brother Faisal, but 100 signed the order to depose Saud seven months later.

TABLE 4
THE SAUDI MONARCHS

King Abdul Aziz Bin Saud, born 1880, ruled 1902-53 (died)
King Saud, born 1902, ruled 1953-64 (deposed; died 1969)
King Faisal, born 1906, ruled 1964-75 (assassinated)
King Khalid, born 1913, ruled 1975-82 (died)
King Fahd, born 1921, ruled 1982-
   Abd Allah—crown prince, next in line (Commander of the
    National Guard)
   Sultan—Second Deputy Prime Minister, second in line
    (Minister of Defense and Aviation)

(A list of all the sons and grandsons of King Abdul Aziz is found in Appendix C.)

The surviving sons of Abdul Aziz have 13 different mothers, who came from the important tribes in the kingdom. Inevitably the sons are tied by blood to and espouse the interests of the groups from which they came. King Fahd is one of seven brothers of a Sudairi mother (along with Sultan, Abd al Rahman, Nayif, Turki, Salman, and Ahmad) mentioned earlier. This group has always encouraged the modernization process and has generally favored strong reciprocal relations with the United States.

The important Shammar tribe is represented by Prince Abd Allah (presently crown prince), son of Al Fahda bint Asi al Shuraym. Her people were a deeply traditional and powerful Bedouin group that spans the northern border of Saudi Arabia with Syria. Abd Allah had no brothers, but has formed close alliances with his half-brothers. Before King Khalid named him second deputy prime minister, he had for some time been commander of the National Guard, still very much a conservative force of Bedouin warriors. He has retained that important command.

The next generation of princes (the grandsons of King Abdul Aziz) is defined by a high level of education (including graduate degrees abroad). They represent a variety of viewpoints, which is expected to enhance the planning and development of the country.

The Intricacies of Succession to the Saudi Throne

The manner in which kings have succeeded each other in Saudi Arabia has reflected the manner in which the Saudi government conducts its affairs. King Abdul Aziz designated his eldest son Saud to succeed him, to be assisted by Faisal, next eldest. In 1960 four of Abdul Aziz's sons were attracted by Egypt's call for radical reforms in the Arab world, and suggested that Saudi Arabia needed a written constitution and a consultative council. Radical Arab politics in Egypt soon led to their disenchantment. History proved that natural evolution eventually prevails in bringing about desired change through wise, well-studied policies.

King Saud was less talented in administration than his illustrious father. Eventually the urgency of state affairs led to his deposition in 1964.

Crown Prince Faisal—humble, honest, pious, thrifty, and attentive to details—was put on the throne without the world ever knowing what internal debates took place within the royal family. Thereafter, competence became as important in the succession as family position, with some princes stepping aside.

King Faisal immediately set about imposing fiscal responsibility in government. He laid down another precedent by passing over the next brother (Muhammad) and naming Khalid crown prince, thus establishing who was to succeed him. King Khalid in turn designated Fahd as crown prince, passing over two older half- brothers. Khalid also named Abd Allah as second deputy prime minister, extending the line of succession.

The method by which these decisions were made remains a private matter, but clearly an institutionalized process now exists within the House of Saud for determining who shall be king. When the succession will pass to the next generation has not yet been indicated.

Appointment of a Council of Ministers

Shortly before his death in 1953, King Abdul Aziz created a Council of Ministers—the first step toward a coherent administration. This body was enlarged under Abdul Aziz's son King Saud (1953-64). His successor, King Faisal (1964-75), focused considerable attention on the modernization of Saudi Arabia's governing institutions.

He decreed that the king would act as prime minister thereafter, directly responsible for all government policies. Local officials were also made responsible to the king. The flow of oil revenue into Saudi Arabia made possible a phenomenal expansion of government services, requiring increases in the number of ministries.

In 1970 King Faisal created a Ministry of Justice to regulate the autonomous religious courts. His other efforts to meld the religious scholars into the bureaucracy included the creation of a Ministry of Pilgrimage Affairs and Religious Trusts, which has the same rank as all other ministries. Government also includes a Committee for the Protection of Virtue and Prevention of Vice, which supervises the religious police.

Very soon after Faisal's death in 1975, his brother King Khalid expanded the number of ministries from 14 to 20—essentially rounding out the modern Saudi administration. The Council of Ministers is not a cabinet or legislature in the Western sense. It is an advisory body, appointed by the king, serving at his discretion, and responsible exclusively to him. Its purpose is to implement policy, but in the absence of a legislature, ministers get involved in making policy as well as through their advice and recommendations to the king.

The Council of Ministers shown in Figure 1.2 is a familiar governing mechanism, for it parallels the administrative structure of any modern nation. Unlike impersonal bureaucracies which are a relatively neutral force in a free enterprise system, the Saudi administration actively manages all the social technology—education, housing, defense, industry, agriculture, natural resources—for the society as a whole.

In addition to their normal functions, several ministries have responsibility in broad technical spheres that might be private enterprise in some other countries—public utilities (either directly or through public corporations), transportation, the petroleum industry, social insurance, and the like. Three ministries are also responsible for the adjudication of non-religious matters.

As vast oil income has been invested in economic diversification, the affairs of the kingdom have become increasingly complex. Ministers become more powerful as their duties expand. Dealing with the day-to-day problems of running the kingdom, studying its successes and failures, they are in the best position to suggest needed changes and recommend new policies to the king. The ministerial bureaucracy has become the framework that supervises the rapidly expanding public sectors in the kingdom.

Although the number of princes from the House of Saud serving in the Council of Ministers gradually declined in the 1970s, leading princes have secured training in statecraft as ministers. King Fahd, for example, was appointed the first Minister of Education when the ministry was created in 1953—laying the foundations of Saudi Arabia's education policy. In 1962 he became Minister of Interior. He established the King Fahd Military College and led delegations to Arab League meetings, as well as to London, Washington, and OPEC. He was named Crown Prince in 1975—all training for assuming the throne seven years later.

Al Saud princes continue to head the key political and military ministries, putting them in a position to make the final decisions in policy matters. By 1984, however, 16 of the 25 members of the Council of Ministers were commoners, many of them technocrats with Ph.D. degrees from American or European universities, who were responsible for supervising the country's economic development.

Figure 2
Council of Ministries

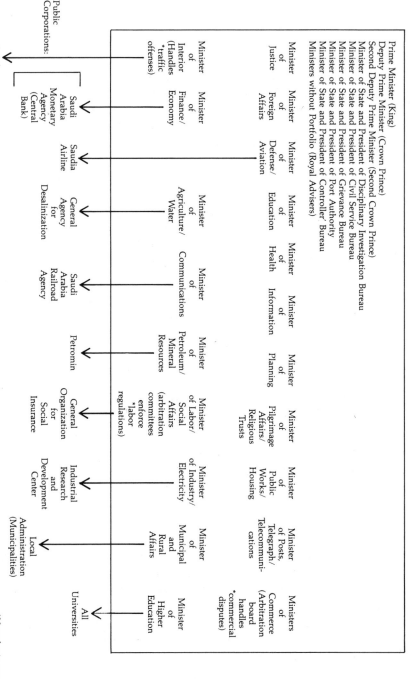

*Non-sharia matters

The Majlis as a Vehicle for Representation

Islam requires that both leaders and citizens should participate in government through a process of consultation. Saudi Arabia has a traditional institution for which there is no equivalent in the West—the king's personal audience *(majlis)*—where any subject of the king can bring an opinion, a grievance, or ask for assistance in almost any matter, and receive immediate attention. The audiences are held in a chamber with no throne or dias. The king's chair differs from the others only in having a telephone, pad, and pencil on a small stand beside it. No pomp or panoply is involved. This informal access to their rulers results in a remarkable closeness between governed and those governing.

King Abdul Aziz made himself accessible at a daily majlis and used it very effectively in commanding devoted loyalty to his highly personal rule. These meetings provided him with invaluable information about prevailing personal rivalries, alliances, and dissatisfactions. At the same time, his subjects felt that this personal access to their ruler gave them a voice in the country's government.

The majlis has traditionally been held at several levels—by the monarch himself or his personal representative (the crown prince or a minister), by all the senior princes and their sons, by leaders of aristocratic families, and by the king's amirs (governors) who represent him in all the provinces. This personal relationship between royal family and the citizens they rule is casual, trusting, affectionate in tenor, and a source of Saudi pride. It replicates the old Bedouin value system where the chief is first among equals. In Saudi eyes, the opportunity to speak personally to their rulers is more valuable than an occasional impersonal vote in an election, and makes elected legislatures unnecessary.

The majlis is the place for the individual citizen to express his personal views, eliminating the need for political parties or labor unions. Nor is a free press considered necessary if every individual has the opportunity to talk directly to the king or to the king's representative.

As population has grown, government increased in complexity, wealth increased rapidly, and Saudi Arabia's economy diversified, the effectiveness of the personal majlis in assessing the mood of the country and permitting direct political participation has decreased. Abdul Aziz's sons have found it necessary to require each supplicant to also present a written petition, which can be studied and answered in a subsequent session. Royal control today is bolstered by power derived from oil wealth as much as by personal contact with Saudi citizens.

The institution known in the Muslim world as majlis can also be a tribal council or a legislative assembly *(majlis al shura)*, generally made up of a country's family and tribal leaders. This kind of majlis has always been held informally by the Saudi kings—regular ad hoc assemblages of leading members of the ruling class (royal family, ulama, tribal shaykhs), where matters of import are discussed informally in search of consensus. King Faisal welcomed such a group in his palace every night at eleven o'clock. In times of crisis, important government officials come together immediately to work out solutions to the problem, as they did when replacing King Saud with King Faisal. The possibility of institutionalizing such a majlis al shura has been discussed at various critical times in Saudi Arabia over the last 30 years.

Constitutional Reform

In 1979, after the seizure of the Grand Mosque by zealous individuals, King Khalid appointed the Minister of Interior, Prince Naif to head a commission to study the creation of a formal majlis. However, the timing did not yet seem right, nor was there a desire among the growing middle class for this body. Some western-educated technocrats might discuss liberalization, but others among the new intelligentsia were deeply committed to Islam and the Saudi way of life and critical of Western institutions and materialism.

Iraq's occupation of Kuwait in 1990 posed a truly major crisis. Saudi Arabia faced Iraqi troops massed on its northern border with small, loyal and manageable armed forces—well-equipped and well-led, but inadequate in numbers to stop any Iraqi thrust to the south. Forty-one countries offered assistance in driving Iraq from Kuwait. (Desert Storm is discussed in Chapter 6).

In February 1992, on the 10th anniversary of his reign, King Fahd stated that the trauma of Iraq's invasion of Kuwait had "made it necessary to develop the country's administrative structure." He issued a decree outlining a Basic Law—the first attempt to codify the unwritten principles on which the monarchy has ruled since the country's founding. These constitutional reforms are divided into seven main chapters: System of Government, Features of the Saudi Family, Economic Principles, Rights and Duties, The Authorities of the State, Financial Affairs, and Regional Authorities. *(Footnote:* Source of Information: *FBIS-NES,* March 2, 1992. *Riyadh Daily Newpaper,* August 21, 1993. *Arab News,* August 24, 1993.

The Statute for Governing reaffirms that Saudi Arabia "is an Arab and Islamic sovereign state, its religion Islam, and its constitution the Holy Quran and teachings of the prophet." It provides for an independent judiciary, but with the proviso that judgments should not contradict the sharia.

The Statute for Governing confirms the present system of monarchy and indicates that rule is collectively handed down by an electoral college of about 500 royal princes. The crown will pass to "the most suitable" person among the sons and grandsons of Abdul Aziz.

The section on economic principles stipulates that all the kingdom's natural wealth is the property of the state. Private property, once granted, is protected except when it is needed for public purposes, for which fair compensation must be paid.

The section on rights and duties promises that the state will protect human rights "in accordance with the Islamic sharia," and specifies protection against arbitrary arrest, forced entry and surveillance "except in cases defined by statutes," and retroactive prosecution.

The Statute for the Consultative Assembly provides for the appointment "from among the best citizens," not less than 30 years of age, of a 61-member advisory council. Members of this majlis al shura will have the right to question ministers, propose laws, and advise the king on a broad range of policy matters, including foreign affairs. Half of the membership is to be changed every four years (except for half of the first group appointed)—a fairly limited term of office. The king has absolute right to dissolve the council.

The council is to set its own internal agenda, and when 10 members agree that a matter must be brought before the king, the council's speaker will do so. Decisions will be by majority vote, with the king to ratify them if approved by the council of ministers. Council members may not hold other government posts or even company directorships unless the king approves. Such a majlis, when it is appointed and called to meet, would exercise the first secular restraint ever placed on the power of the Saudi government, for the new body can introduce and pass legislation which the king approves when the council of ministers agrees. The king has absolute right to dissolve the council.

This will not be an assembly representing all the people in the Western sense. King Fahd stated in an interview with a Kuwaiti newspaper that "the democratic system prevailing in the West does not suit us in this region. . . . The system of free election is not part of Islamic ideology." Such a majlis would, however, for the first time bring into the open a decisionmaking process that has taken place behind closed doors, in some measure supporting consensus politics with majority vote.

King Fahd's decision to create a consultative council has more likelihood of succeeding in the 1990s than in earlier decades. The Saudi population is better-educated today, more aware of national issues, and the traumatic events of the Gulf War have heightened the allegiance of the Saudi people to their homeland.

The section on regional authorities provides for the establishment of appointed provincial councils with limited local authority, an apparent attempt to decentralize many bureaucratic functions of the state. It also specifies the relationships between the branches of government rather than leaving local affairs very much up to the personal discretion or judgment of the particular governor of each province.

King Fahd's new government decrees confirm and demonstrate his proven ability to effectively rule Saudi Arabia. The presentation of the Basic Law of Government, Shura Council Statute Decree and the Decree on Regions Statute affirms the effort of political reform by the Saudi government. Furthermore, these decrees embrace reforms that will positively influence the social environment and economic climate of the Kingdom. The commitment to these programs comes at a time when open deliberation of reform has been appraised and received with great approval by the population of Saudi Arabia. These innovative legislative acts assert and preserve the principles, honor and integrity of the Islamic religion. More recently, King Fahd has already began to enact this plan as he has announced the new sixty member majlis-al-shura, including its' President, Vice President and Secretary General.

*See Appendix A for Actual Text

Religious Law and the Monarchy

The strength of the judiciary in Saudi Arabia derives from the fact that the Quran functions as the kingdom's constitution, with the sharia its legal system. No proselytizing is permitted by other faiths, so no problems of ethnic, religious, or linguistic pluralism exist. Saudi Arabia escaped the imposition of foreign legal systems, so the sharia remains undefiled. It is made up of the Quran, the *sunnah* (sayings and actions of the Prophet), *ijma* (consensus of learned scholars), and *qiyas* (decisions deduced by analogies). Judges *(qadis)* must have spent several years studying the sources of the sharia. Historically, the judiciary in Saudi Arabia has been very independent and is considered to be an extension of the ruling authority in that judges work in conjunction with the ruler.

The dominant function of the sharia is to protect the social order, as well as the rights of individuals. The right of habeas corpus (protection against arbitrary imprisonment) is also reserved by religious law in Saudi Arabia. A 1983 regulation stipulated that an investigation of a criminal charge should be completed within three days of arrest. Foreign governments and foreign contractors must operate under Saudi law within the kingdom, which does not necessarily coincide with legal systems abroad.

These are minor concerns to the Saudis. They care more about the rule of law and the strict enforcement of discipline. Saudis believe crime should be swiftly punished, and a penal system where the proscribed punishments fit the values of the society deters citizens from offending against its laws. To be effective, punishment should bring shame on a criminal and satisfy the honor of the wronged persons' family. Saudis often point out with pride that the crime rate in the kingdom is very low, compared with other countries. Other factors may enter, but the system of punishment is clear and unambiguous and serves as a powerful deterrent.

Punishment for crime, laid down in the Quran, is very explicit, and all criminal cases must be dealt with under due process of law. The sentence of the court is subject to a comprehensive appeals procedure. Murderers and rapists are publicly executed. (The West may execute murderers, but often lets rapists off with a slap on the wrist—showing less respect for women's rights than sharia.) The penalty for proven adultery can be death, but four witnesses must testify to having seen the adultery to prove that it occurred. A couple must flaunt their behavior to be punished.

Repeated thievery can lead to amputation of the hands or public flogging. Alcohol is prohibited because it is a drug which wastes financial resources better spent on necessities, and leads to civil offenses and criminal acts (e.g., violence in the home, civil disturbances, motoring offenses, sexual offenses, and the like).

The Religious Scholars

The *ulama* (religious scholars) in Saudi Arabia number in the thousands, and include religious students, judges, lawyers, seminary teachers, and the prayer leaders (imams) of the mosques. They are considered the guardians of the Islamic value system. King Fahd meets regularly with top ulama, and requests their advice for important decisions, legitimizing actions the king wishes to take.

A Supreme Judicial Council (Council of Senior Ulama) was created by King Faisal in 1971 to advise him on religious matters and sanction the king's decisions—his way of incorporating the ulama into the state bureaucracy. This Council interprets the sharia, supervises the judges (qadi) of the lower courts, whom it nominates for appointment by the king, and examines death sentences passed by the lower courts. It makes rulings on all kinds of secular matters. These rulings give legitimacy to the development process and to government policies. Approval of this body was considered essential both in 1979 when dissidents were driven from the Grand Mosque in Makkah, and in 1990 when foreign troops were permitted into the kingdom to liberate Kuwait.

This group of the most prominent religious scholars in the kingdom advises the Minister of Justice, who is himself one of the country's most senior ulama and serves as chief of the Supreme Judicial Council. The modern descendants of Muhammad bin Abd al Wahhab—the Al Shaykh family—hold some important religious and legal posts in the kingdom, symbolizing the historical alliance between the religious reformers and the Al Saud family.

The composition of the Supreme Council changes from time to time, with younger scholars of a more progressive outlook on the relationship between religion and the modernization of the nation replacing older ulama with uncompromisingly conservative views. These changes stem from the government's determination to proceed cautiously with constitutional reform.

In addition to advising the Minister of Justice and supervising the courts, the ulama control girls' education, the Religious Guidance Department, three Islamic universities, the Great Mosques, and the Organization for Promoting Good and Discouraging Evil (which supervises the public morality committees).

The Court System

The king is the highest court of appeal. Below the king are two courts of appeal (one in Riyadh, one in Makkah), consisting of a panel of several qadis. Summary courts are courts of the first instance, with jurisdiction limited to minor criminal and civil matters. Generally, a single qadi hears cases. High courts handle all cases that are beyond the jurisdiction of the summary courts. Very serious criminal cases are heard by three qadis of the high court.

ADJUDICATION IN SHARIA COURTS

An accused man is innocent until proven guilty. The burden of proof falls upon the plaintiff. No juries exist.

The plaintiff and defendant sit together on a bench directly in front of the qadi (judge). The judge's role is not to arbitrate, but to actively seek the truth and render justice. Procedures are as simple as possible so that an ordinary man may bring his complaint and receive a fair hearing. Both parties and all witnesses are questioned by the judge, not by lawyers. The judge decides the integrity of the witnesses, and may ask for character witnesses to help him. Each party may cross-examine the other party and his witnesses. The judge may reach a compromise decision if he is in doubt as to which party is in the right.

Two types of action may be brought—a public right action (the State charges a violation of public law) and a private right action (an individual seeks redress for a wrong). The same trial may deal with both. The qadi will determine fault and prescribe the compensatory damages to be paid under a private right action, as well as define the punishment to be imposed under a public right action. Or he may mediate a satisfactory compromise between the parties. He may also recommend clemency in any case brought before him.

To prove his case, the plaintiff must produce two eye witnesses to establish his claim. If he cannot, then he can demand an oath from the defendant that he did not do that with which he is charged. Refusal by the defendant to make the oath results in an automatic guilty verdict. What is to prevent his lying? Perjury, when proven to the satisfaction of the judge, is punishable by imprisonment or lashing, or both. Furthermore, Muslims believe that God knows when a man lies, and punishment will come at the final judgment.

Islamic law has been applied since the establishment of the kingdom in strict accordance with the interpretation of the Hanbali school of Sunni Islam, which emphasizes tradition rather than speculative material in its interpretations. It does, however, maintain that "things are assumed to be allowable unless there is proof of their prohibition." Saudi kings have, therefore, issued numerous codes (nizam) to meet modern development needs. These codes have introduced radio and television, made possible modern contracts, and regulated bureaucratic procedures not detailed by sharia.

Secular organs have been established to deal with issues outside the sharia court system. The Board of Grievances, an independent bureau under the Presidency of the Council of Ministers, hears administrative cases brought against government officials and qadis. Motor vehicle regulations are enforced by special police in the Ministry of Interior. Commercial disputes are subject to arbitration by a board in the Ministry of Commerce. Labor regulations are enforced by special committees in the Ministry of Labor and Social Affairs.

Local Administration

Saudi Arabia is a nation forged of numerous regions, each of which was once ruled by a tribal shaykh. King Abdul Aziz traveled around his kingdom, consulting the shaykhs on their opinions. Difficult transportation and communication, however, permitted local rulers considerable autonomy.

In 1975 the kingdom was organized into 14 provinces, each with a governor (amir) appointed by the king. Governors in populous provinces may be assisted by a deputy. The governors are often sons or grandsons of King Abdul Aziz, and usually report directly to the king, although they may deal directly with the ministries as they see fit. Since other local officials are responsible to ministries, some uncertainty has existed as to the exact chain of command, which may be corrected by the new Statue for the Provinces. At present, the amirs coordinate local functions.

The major responsibility of the governor is the maintenance of security within the province through control of the local police and National Guard units. The governor oversees the activities of central government agencies (the Ministries of Planning, Education, Public

Works and Housing, Industry and Electricity, Agriculture and Water), and supervises municipal officials within his province. One of his prime responsibilities is to hear the petitions of local citizens in his public majlis, arbitrating disputes himself or referring them to the appropriate court. This gives every citizen the opportunity to express his opinions directly to a responsible official.

TABLE 5
THE FOURTEEN PROVINCES OF SAUDI ARABIA

Province	Capital
Riyadh	Riyadh
Makkah Al-Mukarramah	Makkah (Mecca)
Madinah Al-Munawarah	Madinah (Medina)
Asir	Abha
Eastern Region	Dammam
Hail	Hail
Northern Border Region	Ar'ar
Qassim (Qasim)	Buraidah (Buraydah)
Najran	Najran
Al Baha	Al Baha
Jizan	Jizan
Tabouk	Tabouk (Tabuk)
Al Jouf	Shaka
Qirayyat (Qurayat)	Qirayyat (Qurayat)

Source: Ministry of Information

Only in the late 1970s was local administration standardized throughout the kingdom, making local officials of districts and sub-districts responsible to the Minister of Interior, as shown in Figure 1.2 Council of Ministers Chart (on page 47). Officials at the municipal level report to the Ministry of Municipal and Rural Affairs (established in 1975 to replace a deputy minister in the Ministry of Interior), although they may answer as well to the local governor. Mayors, sometimes assisted by municipal managers, are the chief officials in towns and villages. Municipal officials see to the implementation of local ordinances, collect fees, protect public health and safety, license construction and professionals, improve public infrastructure, supervise local goods and services, and control prices.

National Security

Before the Gulf War the Saudi defense organization was small and fragmented into five organizations with little coordination: The Royal Saudi Army, Royal Saudi Air Force, and Royal Saudi Navy were formed to protect the nation and were supervised by the minister of defense and aviation. The Saudi Arabian National Guard was the military division of the Presidency of the Council of Ministers. The Frontier Forces and Coast Guard were supervised by the minister of the interior.

The National Guard was created after the 1929 Ikhwan revolt to secure the support of the tribes by providing them with employment and incomes. It was strengthened in the 1950s and 1960s as a mechanism for maintaining internal security.

Both the armed forces and the National Guard are headed by very senior princes, and key command positions are filled by members of the royal family and other Saudi professionals. Officers and troops for the armed forces are drawn from the urban middle class. Trained Saudis make competent officers, but the lower ranks and maintenance personnel are more difficult to recruit. Because the armed forces are a potential breeding ground for discontent, the government tries to keep them out of the political arena. Air Force officers, who are the elite of the defense establishment, are drawn from the best of the military recruits. They are usually graduates of the best Western aviation and military academies.

Major attention was directed to the Saudi armed forces in the 1960s, when they were doubled to offset the threat of radical Arab regimes in Egypt, Syria, and Iraq. Because the kingdom's sparse population was inadequate to defend its huge territory, emphasis was focused on high-tech equipment for air force and air defenses to hold off any attack until outside help could arrive.

Avoidance of armed conflict has been a major objective of the Saudi government. Though well-trained and equipped, its armed forces are not adequate to defend such a large land mass. Although security agreements with other nations have provided a measure of assurance, Saudi leaders prefer diplomacy and negotiation to the use of force.

Unrest inside the kingdom in 1969-70 led to a stepping up of security forces. Military forces are often a potent spur for change in developing countries, because they are one of the few cohesive groups in society supervised by well-educated officers, often trained in the West. The military in Saudi Arabia has, however, always remained loyal to its country.

The armed forces were upgraded and equipped with sophisticated modern weapons in the 1980s, although still kept small and manageable. They came into their own during the Gulf War (which is discussed in Chapter 6). Today a large portion of the kingdom's budget is spent on defense.

CONSENSUS MONARCHY AS A GOVERNING MECHANISM

King Abdul Aziz Ibn Saud is revered as the father of his country. His highly personal rule, extending through the network of alliances and marriages by which he unified the country, gave him an intimate knowledge of his people and their problems. His accessibility promoted their loyalty; his piety and respect for the ulama won their admiration. And his great physical courage and consummate skill as a warrior permitted him to subdue those whom he could not win by guile or affection.

King Abdul Aziz set the ruling style for Saudi Arabia. His sons have continued his paternal rule, but in vastly different economic circumstances. All the kingdom's wealth has come from resource revenues rather than from taxes.

The power structure draws much of its strength from a vast network of alliances among all the important groups in the country, integrated through regular formal and informal consultation between Saudi rulers and their colleagues. A large amount of discussion and debate can take place in this manner. But the Saudi rulers are groping for ways to institutionalize the traditional custom of personal consultation—at the municipal, district, provincial, and national levels—so that increasing numbers of citizens feel that their voices are both heard and heeded.

Assimilating the Technocrats

Educated Saudis, whether royal or commoners, have been brought into the government at every level and have replaced the traditional tribal chiefs as the country's elite. Security and religious affairs remain firmly in the control of the Saudi government, but appointments to high positions in nearly every other sphere have increasingly depended on education and ability, rather than on social status. This represents a move away from traditional society, where rewards are a function of status, toward industrial society, where rewards determine status.

This utilization of all the kingdom's talents has linked the new technocrats to the monarchy. Bureaucratic inefficiencies in the late 1970s made it clear that practical experience must also be a criterion for government appointments, and today's students are encouraged to study and gain experience in subjects vital to the kingdom's development.

Satisfying the Tribes

The tribes have lost much of their economic and political functions, and serve now as social units, dependent on the monarchy for financial subsidies. They are now by and large settled in towns, although many nomads have refused to move into new apartment blocks because no space was provided for keeping animals, and the nomads are reluctant to give up the freedom of what they consider a superior lifestyle.

Alliances and compromises between the royal family and tribal leaders are less necessary in keeping government functioning. Tribal leaders cannot help but be aware of their demotion on the social scale by the settled bureaucrats and technocrats of the towns, but loyalty among the chiefs to the Al Saud family remains strong. Control of oil wealth gives the government the economic power to provide generous subsidies and services, generally keeping the tribes contented.

Government control of oil wealth also eliminates the need for taxing the citizenry. The tribes are dependent on the government for subsidies; the citizens for social services. The shaykhs' role now focuses on settling minor disputes or arbitrating conflicts; giving advice on location of schools, roads, clinics, and the like; explaining government agricultural plans to the people; identifying those in need of social services; and keeping track of immigrants whose visas expire. The role of the tribal chief might be further institutionalized by assigning clear duties and by requiring a certain level of education as well as training in local regulations and fixing the level of fees for their services.

Mollifying the Fanatical Leaders

The real modernization of Saudi Arabia began under King Faisal, whose well-known piety made him secure enough in his Islamic credentials to bring the judiciary into the formal system of government. The influence of the ulama continued, however, particularly after a fanatic religious group seized the holiest shrine of Islam, the Grand Mosque in Makkah, on the first day of A.H. 1400 (October 1979). The leader of the insurrection, Juhaiman bin Muhammad bin Saif al Utaibi, was an authentic Saudi from a major Bedouin tribe. He and his 250 followers claimed to be the successors to the Ikhwan, accusing the people of being subverted by Western culture while making hypocritical public displays of piety, and the moderate religious scholars who supported the government of being tainted with the same poison. They wanted to overthrow the government and return Saudi Arabia to what they called the true faith.

They were disappointed in their belief that the Saudi population would rally behind them. The religious scholars were not sympathetic to this rebellion. The general reaction among the people was shock at the defiling of Islam's holiest shrine. After two weeks, top religious scholars advised that the army, National Guard, and police should storm the site. All the rebels were killed or captured, with subsequent public executions.

King Khalid, convinced that a balance must be preserved between conservatives and modernists, appointed a member of the Al Shaykh family (direct descendants of Muhammad ibn Abd al Wahhab) to be Minister of Justice, to hold weekly consultations with the ulama. He also decided the time was appropriate to make rules of conduct stricter. The sexes were strictly separated in schools and the proportion of required religious courses in the curriculum increased.

King Fahd, who succeeded King Khalid, understood the importance of the monarch's public image. He also brought enlightened ulama into his cabinet and gave them expanded responsibilities in order to integrate them into the Saudi establishment, without interfering in politics, foreign affairs, or economic development. Numerous royal decrees have demanded strict adherence to the Islamic moral code, enforcement of daily prayers, and the like.

The carefully constructed networks of support which the government has woven throughout Saudi society mesh well with the kingdom's traditions and are crucial to the enhancement of the present system.

Intensive development over the past decade has changed the face of Saudi cities, helping transform them into bustling centers of urban, commercial and industrial activity.

Modern architecture distinguishes Saudi Arabia's major cities, for example Jiddah, the bustling Red Sea port and commercial metropolis seen (above). Upper right corner: Minarets of the Sacred Mosque loom behind modern apartment buildings in Mecca. Hospitals and clinics, supported by modern laboratories (below) provide advanced health care and services.

Chapter 4
SAUDI CULTURE AND CHARACTER

Two significant characteristics distinguish Saudi Arabia from the ranks of Third World countries that are struggling to achieve self-sustaining growth. Because there was little in Saudi Arabia to attract the intrusion of colonial powers, the country was never subjected to pervasive outside control and so never adopted patterns from other cultures. The Saudis have never considered rejecting their Islamic heritage in favor of an alien philosophy. They have moved into the modern era with considerable assurance as to their own identity.

Also, the development process in the kingdom is taking place in the context of enormous wealth, giving Saudi Arabia definite advantages over much poorer and more populous developing countries. The national psychology in Saudi Arabia is one of fierce pride and independence, rather than anger over economic exploitation by foreign powers. Substantial revenue assures endless opportunities for advancement for educated Saudis, both in government and in the private sector.

Oil wealth disbursed through a patrimonial tribal organization has permitted the Saudis to build sophisticated modern infrastructure before popular demands escalated more rapidly than they could be satisfied. The government has financed roads, railroads, airlines, power grids, telecommunications, and extensive social services for all its citizens. Education, medicine, and health care services are free to all. Pensions are provided to widows, the elderly, and the permanently disabled. Aid is available to victims of natural disasters and those who are temporarily disabled. Interest-free loans are provided for home mortgages, construction, small business, and agricultural development.

Adjustments to Change Accompany Modernization

Modernization brings, however, rapid urbanization, a better-educated population, heightened political awareness because communications have grown, and elevated materialistic expectations. The Saudi rulers have striven to invest their huge oil revenues in massive economic development while at the same time warding off the impact of rapid change on their customs and traditions.

Woe to every (kind of) scandal-monger and backbiter, who pileth up wealth and layeth it by, thinking that his wealth would make him last forever.

By no means! He will be sure to be thrown into that which Breaks to Pieces.

And what will explain to thee That which Breaks to Pieces?

(It is) the Fire of (the Wrath of) God kindled (to a blaze), the which doth mount (right) to the Hearts.

Qur'an: CIV, 1-7

The great changes that have taken place in the last twenty-five years as a result of a startling infusion of oil wealth have occurred in too short a time to negate the Bedouin ethos of Arabia and the traditional values of Islam. Religion is a very constant presence in daily life in the kingdom, visible not only in the regular prayer ritual which brings all other activity to a halt five times a day, but in multiple tiny reminders that punctuate every activity. God's name is invoked in almost every statement a Saudi makes because he believes his whole destiny is already known to God. Every public announcement and every government document begins with the words, "In the name of God, the Merciful, the Compassionate." Even the airplane stewardess who announces, "We will land in a few minutes," adds "God willing," to her statement.

Many Saudis are considered members of a current class called *salafiyya*, that is, thinkers who respect the life and thought of the *salaf*—that earliest generation of Muslims who declared the Quran and hadith the only valid foundation for Muslim life. Today the Saudi *Salafi* are attempting to harmonize the complex needs of modern life with ancient religious law. The Quran states that the gaining of knowledge is the highest religious activity, one that is most pleasing in God's eyes. Educating women—a very forward-looking concept—is, for example, one of the government's central concerns. At the same time, they are determined to avoid the crass materialism and social malaise that have resulted from the secular preoccupations in the West.

> ...So eat and drink of the sustenance provided by God, and do no evil nor mischief on the (face of the) earth.
>
> *Qur'an: II, 60*

FAMILY AS THE FOUNDATION OF SAUDI SOCIETY

Family ties determine the structure of society throughout Saudi Arabia, an inheritance from the days when the nomadic clan was the basic social and economic unit in a hostile desert environment. Close-knit families, working together to tend their flocks and move them from pasture to pasture, were essential to survival. Coupled with the organization of society on kinship lines is the long-accepted regulation of family, clan, and tribal life by Muslim law, so that a strong ethical imperative strengthens family and kin affiliations and mutual obligations.

Close Ties Among and Obligations to the Extended Family

In anthropological terms, the Arabian family is patriarchal, patrilineal, patrilocal, endogamous, and occasionally polygamous. Its nucleus is not just father, mother, and children, but all the brothers of one generation, their wives and children, grandparents, possibly some elderly aunts and uncles, and occasionally some cousins who have no family to care for them. These family units are organized around closely related males, with descent traced through the father's side of the family and captured in each individual's name. A male name is followed by *bin* or *ibn, meaning "son of," and his father's name; a woman's name by bint*, meaning "daughter of." The family unit is the source of identity for each individual in it. Family obligations come before all others. One always supports one's kin in a quarrel with any outsider.

A Saudi family lives together, and social life takes place within kinship groups. Family members are unaccustomed to spending time alone, but are always surrounded by relatives. They do not isolate themselves spatially, but only by silence. No family member is left in need; taking care of one's relatives—sometimes referred to as nepotism in Western cultures—is considered a virtue.

The Saudis who are nomadic herdsmen make their homes in a cluster of tents set up beside a well or spring. If they are settled farmers, their home is a series of interconnected rooms which face away from the road onto a central courtyard. City dwellers may enjoy a house or apartment which houses only part of an extended family, but even these maintain close ties with their kin in the village from which they originally came.

City dwellers also continue many of the customs of their Bedouin ancestors, such as having separate living areas where men and women socialize apart from each other. Cushions and bolsters on the floor of such rooms replicate the atmosphere of informality in the desert tent. Beautiful Persian carpets that served as furniture and sleeping mats in Bedouin tents now grace the floors of apartments, villas, and sun-dried block dwellings. Every guest is made to feel immediately at ease as he joins the relaxed family circle sitting on cushions on the floor. One cannot feel stiff or formal in this posture. Much warmth and swift acceptance of outsiders is lost when Arabs put European furniture into their living rooms, for social contacts then become more formal, and the easy assimilation of guests into a delightful fellowship is diminished.

The open warmth of the Saudi Arabs also derives from their nomadic background. In a harsh desert landscape the traveler on the move is apt to be dependent on the next individual he meets for some essential—food, water, shelter, or transport. From such interdependence comes immediate acceptance and a willingness to reveal frankly who you are, where you came from, where you are going, and what news you picked up on the way. The same kind of quick acceptance and concern for one's fellow man characterized the frontier society of the American West, where the kindness one extended to a stranger was reciprocated by the next person, and the willingness to lend a helping hand was often crucial to a stranger's progress and survival.

The Saudis carry this concept of hospitality even further and consider it their duty to make a guest welcome, to offer him sustenance and security. Even an enemy must be protected for at least three days, because no one could survive in the desert by cunning alone, but required food and water. Thus a man in flight can seek respite in the camp of his enemies; a woman can put herself into the hands of strangers; and a traveler can leave his possessions with people he has never seen before. All feel honor bound to care for a stranger's needs.

Awareness of and Pride in Lineages

Families are grouped into clans, composed of several extended families who are related to one another by descent from a common male ancestor several generations earlier. Related clans who recognize ties to each other consider themselves part of an even larger kin unit, the tribe. Some tribes are very small, consisting of only a few clans; others are very large, and enjoy considerable power and prestige. No matter how nebulous one's ancestry may be or how far removed from tribal life, all Saudis can tell you which of the over 80 major Arabian tribes they belong to, and the fact of belonging is a source of pride and an obligation to aid fellow tribesmen.

Among the nomadic herdsmen, of course, the tribal structure continues intact today, for related clans still move together seeking grasslands for their animals, and pitch their tent camps in clusters near a water source during the dry season. Each clan is headed by a *shaykh*, chosen usually from a particular family which has the hereditary right to lead the clan. The individual whom the male heads of the families in the clan choose as their leader is, however, the person whom they trust and believe has leadership qualities, and he serves by their consent and can be replaced if he fails to live up to their expectations. The shaykh consults with the other clan elders, and based on their advice makes decision for the whole clan, settles disputes, and represents the tribe in relations with other tribes and with the central government. A combination of clans into a tribe will be headed by one tribal chief—a shaykh who is the consensus choice of all the clan leaders.

The shaykh holds regular *majlis*, gathering together family heads and clan spokesmen to conduct tribal business and air complaints. Before modern government was instituted, a traditional shaykh or *amir* (another title for a tribal leader) and his male relatives were expected to protect the community and maintain law, while the ruler expected his subjects to obey his decisions and to mobilize occasionally to confront a crisis.

Village organization is also based on kinship ties. Small villages consist of one related clan, living close together, tending fields and herds cooperatively, perhaps exchanging animal products with nomads who come regularly to the village to trade for staple food and manufactured items needed in the desert. A village headman will be chosen from a leading family, and he too will meet regularly with the men of the village in open council to manage village affairs and assign community duties. The village will have a public well, a mosque, a marketplace (suq), some small shops, a government school and a clinic, perhaps a public tea house where men may gather.

In larger villages several related clans will be grouped together, each unit living in dwellings placed close together, perhaps giving their name to that particular section of the village. In addition to the village headman and the *imam* (religious leader) of the mosque, a *qadi* will hear cases involving interpretation of the sharia. The headman will hold an appointment from the central government, for today he is part of a national administration which makes him responsible to the amir in the next higher administrative unit in his region.

Modern economic activities have led to the settlement of new villages where unrelated kin groups may be found living together— around pump stations along the oil pipelines which carry petroleum to various ports, or in agricultural development schemes, or in workers' towns in the oil fields. Here economic activity plays a much larger role in giving residents their identity and status than is the rule in traditional settlements.

Larger towns, of course, consist of many unrelated kin groups, but here again the extended family is the fundamental unit of society, and relations are maintained within larger kin groups. A town will have a small group of prominent families of high status who are involved in governing and religious activities as well as in the direction of the economic, manufacturing, trading, and commercial activities of the community. The towns are linked to the central administration by the appointment of officials from the prominent families who are responsible for smaller village units in their region, and are in turn responsible to higher officials in central government ministries.

A town will have its public wells, marketplace, shops, cafes, mosques, clinic, and government school, as well as police and fire posts, playgrounds, a youth center, and a public library. Places of public entertainment are not found; leisure and entertainment take place within the home and are an integral part of family routine—particularly for women. Television has rapidly become the favorite family pastime, with music and videotapes becoming increasingly available in the larger towns.

GROUP ENTERTAINMENT

In 1990 there were 7 Arabic-language newspapers, 3 English-language newspapers, 14 weekly news magazines, and 12 periodicals published in Saudi Arabia. 3.75 million television sets played in the 2.8 million Saudi households, receiving programs from 2 T.V. stations, 4 million radio receivers picked up 43 AM stations and 23 FM stations.

Radio and TV networks, controlled by the government, were developed to keep Saudis informed of government positions and policies, to promote national loyalties, and to convey traditional values. From 10 to 25 percent of programming is religious, depending on the city of origin. An English-language TV channel was introduced in 1983 to entertain foreign workers and help Saudis understand the outside world. English and French news broadcasts are presented daily.

The adoption of any modern technology has ripple effects in a traditional culture such as that of Saudi Arabia. Radio necessitated a switch from the traditional system of tying time to the setting of the sun and the call to evening prayers, to the use of Greenwich Mean Time +3.

No public cinema is permitted because of Islam's emphasis on moral conduct and the dubious moral quality of much Western film. Videotapes are popular in the home, permitting parents to decide what is appropriate for their families.

Festival occasions are celebrated with a great deal of enthusiasm—weddings, circumcisions, birthdays, and religious holidays—and include feasting, group dancing, oral recitations, and musical renditions of epic ballads. Public celebrations are held in every community on two important religious holidays—Id al Adha, which is the feast of sacrifice during the pilgrimage, and Id al Fitr, the feast at the breaking of the fast at the end of Ramadan.

Sporting events such as soccer and horse and camel racing are popular among the men. Wealthy Arabs enjoy hunting with falcons, yachting along the coasts, and owning and racing the small, fast Arabian horse, which is a status symbol in this part of the world.

The emphasis on membership in a family unit leads naturally to strong emphasis on community interests. Islamic law gives precedence to communal interests over those of the individual, and restricts the rights of individuals when they conflict with those of others. Man is enjoined by the Quran to do good, to discharge his duties responsibly, and to not cause harm.

Serve God, and join not any partner with Him; and do good—to parents, kinsfolk, orphans, those in need, neighbors who are near, neighbors who are strangers, the Companion by your side, the way-farer (ye meet), and what your right hands possess.

Qur'an: IV, 36

RELATIONS BETWEEN MEN AND WOMEN

Probably no area of custom puzzles outsiders more than the status of Saudi women and their relationship to their fathers and husbands. Saudi Arabia is still a male-oriented society, with the family the fundamental and universal social unit. Saudi Arabia's five kings have been accessible to the public, but never their wives. According to the teachings of Islam, women should play their role inside the home—as mothers, wives, sisters, and daughters.

Men are the protectors and maintainers of women, because God has given the one more (strength) than the other, and because they support them from their means. Therefore the righteous women are devoutly obedient, and guard in (the husband's) absence what God would have them guard.

Qur'an: IV, 34

All Saudi women live in the households of their male relatives. They are trained from childhood to be wives and mothers and to center their activities in the home, devoting a large part of their attention to the stability of the family. In that realm they have authority equal to men. Because the private sphere is far more dominant than the public in Saudi Arabia, women wield much more power than is visible to the outside world. They are the "matchmakers and the peacemakers," both significant functions where family is the foundation of society and politics are played out behind the scenes.

The Saudi husband is expected to make decisions for his family in all activities and obligations outside the home, but the wife is in charge of the household and reigns supreme within the family walls. She is responsible for the children, daughters-in-law, servants, and even for the men themselves in important family matters. Muslim women have left their mark intellectually as well—as transmitters of hadith, calligraphers, and poets.

Bachelors and spinsters are very rare; everyone is expected to marry. Women who are divorced return to their father's house. Widows become the responsibility of their brothers-in-law.

CLOTHING IN SAUDI ARABIA

Outdoor clothing continues traditional, even in the cities. Although Arabs who come to Saudi Arabia from other Arab countries wear European-style clothing, Saudis dress in the ankle-length white shirt called a thobe *(thawb)* and the large square head scarf called a *gutra*, held in place by a black cord called an agal (aigal, iqal). The agal was originally a double loop of rope a bedouin used to hobble camels, and was stored on his head when not in use.

This costume is practical for hot, dry climates, for the thobe is loose and lets air circulate while it shields the skin from the burning sun, and the gutra shelters the head and keeps out both heat and blowing sand. Over the thobe in cooler weather is worn a long flowing woolen cloak called *aba* or *bisht*. This costume is identical for all Saudi men, with the white head covering predominating in the summer and the red-and-white in the winter. Clothing offers few clues to indicate an individual's economic status or social position, except for the quality of the material from which the agal and outer cloak are made.

Women wear a long black outer cloak (abbayah) over their garments when they are on the street or in public places in Saudi Arabia, with a black chiffon veil over their faces. Like that of the men, this public garment gives no clue to economic status or social position. Under the abbayah, however, may be anything from the most elegant Paris fashion to blue jeans. Modesty requires that the arms and legs are covered.

Male attitudes are shaped by custom and by the venerated Bedouin traits—bravery, honor, stoicism, and hospitality. Men tend to dress alike as a statement of their equality in the eyes of God. The modern Saudi still maintains his close ties with and membership in his extended family and his egalitarian attitude toward his fellow man. He shakes hands with everyone he meets, regardless of rank, and the lowliest employee sits down comfortably with his employer to chat, drink tea, or share a meal. He lines up with other men to pray without any awareness of rank.

The late King Faisal embodied many of the qualities most admired in Saudi men. He is said to have memorized the Quran by the age of ten; learned to ride, fence, and shoot; enjoyed the royal sport of falconry. When he became king, he chastised an assembly in Riyadh for calling him "Your Majesty," saying that Majesty is reserved for God alone. He never sat apart from his subjects. Faisal pointed out that every human being is a servant of God, who alone is worthy of a throne. King Fahd prefers to be addressed as Custodian of the Holy Mosques, rather than by any other title. Saudi kings are buried in unmarked graves to prevent the veneration of the tombs of saintly persons so common in other Muslim countries.

O ye who believe! Enter into Islam whole- heartedly; and follow not the footsteps of the Evil One; for he is to you an avowed enemy. If ye backslide after the clear (Signs) have come to you, then know that God is exalted in Power, Wise. Will they wait until God comes to them in canopies of clouds, with angels (in His train) and the question is (thus) settled? But to God do all questions go back (for decision).

Qur'an: II, 208-10.

The Importance of Personal Honor

The Arabians put great store by self-respect, which derives from the great stress the Bedouin placed on personal honor. This concept of honor is not internalized, but is rather the collective responsibility of the whole family, and is based on their perception of how others view them. Any impingement on personal honor results in shame, in loss of face. Self-respect requires that appearances be preserved at all costs. The defense of personal honor was integrated into the Muslim belief system as a symbol of righteousness.

The deterioration of family stability and values so evident in the West reinforces the Saudi perception that their culture is worth defending. They see a connection between the weakening of family ties in the West and increasing social instability, soaring crime rates, rampant materialism, and the erosion of moral standards. The oil boom has brought increasing crime to Saudi Arabia, in spite of its being one of the strictest law-and-order societies in the world. The Saudis deplore this trend, and often blame the corrupting influence of expatriots working in the kingdom.

Although social distinctions exist in Saudi society, there is no rigid caste system, and businessmen and government employees enjoy a high degree of upward mobility. Capable members of the royal family receive important appointments, but other slots are filled by talented commoners. The country's pressing needs have led to an increasing appreciation for advancement by merit.

The customs and traditions that have shaped the attitudes of the Saudis can create difficulties, however, in adjusting to their changing situation. Saudi honor requires strict conformity to the ethics of the society and is bound up in preserving their traditions. The compulsion to maintain face in public can conflict with efficiency or rapid accomplishment of specific goals. Fear of failure can lead to prevarication and can paralyze decision making. The focus on the externals of behavior often results in superficial accommodations and ephemeral courtesy which are not backed up by determined, concerted action. The belief in predestination can lead to improvidence and derail long-range planning.

Beleaguered officials may blame their troubles on outside forces—not accept them as personal responsibility. Such attitudes do not mesh with the requirements of a modern economy, and are gradually being modified as Saudis assume responsibility for demanding managerial and technological activities and the many services that support those activities.

Traditional patterns of thought are deeply ingrained, however, and when they come into conflict with the requirements of a modernizing economy, they cause the educated Saudi to feel an uneasy ambivalence. He admires Western gadgetry and ideas, but cherishes his own Arab heritage and finds it difficult to reconcile age-old attitudes with the demands of technology.

Many Middle Easterners entertain an ingrained fatalism, thanking God for good things and blaming the bad on influences beyond their control. Some believe that their affairs are being manipulated today by forces hostile to the Arabs. This sense that everything that happens is predestined would seem to make it unnecessary to be provident or plan far ahead, yet no country can invest billions of petrodollars without a great deal of careful advance planning.

The Saudi's attitude toward work is also an inheritance from his Bedouin ancestors, who regarded tending flocks of animals and raiding as honorable professions and menial labor as demeaning. Consequently, thousands of foreign workers have been brought in to do the menial tasks. They come because they can earn more in Saudi Arabia than in their homelands, yet their options are limited by strict Saudi law. They cannot apply for citizenship or purchase land. They can be asked to leave at any time. When they are no longer needed, they are expected to leave.

Many, however, adapt well, enjoy their work and the atmosphere in the kingdom, and stay in the country for decades, even after they have accumulated enough wealth to return to their homelands. Thousands of Americans have positive memories of their years in Saudi Arabia.

Marriage

Islam permits a man to have up to four wives. Wealthy men have more than one wife when they can afford to provide separate quarters for each and treat each equally. The trend, however, is toward monogamy, for most men cannot afford the expense or the effort of more than one household.

Marriage in Islam is a simple civil contract, not a sacrament, and either partner may include conditions in the contract. Marriage customs vary widely in Muslim countries. In Saudi Arabia men set great store on the pre-marital chastity of their wives and fidelity within marriage. The age-old customs of veiling, the seclusion of women, and the strict segregation of the sexes is closely tied into concepts of family honor, for which male members of the family are responsible. These customs also stem from the ancient need in a harsh environment for the individual—male or female—to subordinate his/her needs to the collective interests of the family, clan, or tribe in order to survive. In such a setting, the home and family were women's responsibility, and a woman's status depended on how many sons she produced—an attitude left over from the time when the number of males born was a critical factor in the survival of the Bedouin tribe. Sons are still highly valued.

Marriage is usually arranged by the parents. The prospective husband makes a bridal payment to the girl's father, which is used to buy jewelry, clothing, and articles for her prospective home, or livestock and other property which will serve as an investment for her future security. It may help defray the expenses of the wedding festivities. A man whose wife insists on a divorce or who deserts him may demand the return of his bridal payment, which is strong incentive for families to persuade their daughters to stay with their husbands.

Arranged marriages might seem to ignore personal feelings, but they tend to work out because marriage partners are usually closely related or at least share very similar backgrounds. Well-educated Saudis will tell you that because Saudi boys and girls are taught to respect each other, their marriages develop greater harmony and lasting affection than those based on passionate romantic attachments. Kindness and consideration are highly esteemed virtues in relations between husband and wife. Because both Saudi men and women have traditionally found companionship and intellectual stimulation among members of the same sex, they have not sought these qualities in marriage partners. The rapid increase in university education for both sexes may change this.

A wife leaves her family to live with her husband's kin, but maintains ties to her own parents, and her personal conduct continues to reflect on her father's reputation. In order to maintain family status, or to keep bloodlines pure, or to preserve family property intact, marriages are often arranged within the kin group, preferably between children of brothers or other male relatives.

Often marriage ties are of considerable political importance, both in cementing alliances between clans and in the gathering of important information that is not available to men in their public roles. The wives of senior members of ruling families are often the route through which many members of the community approach the shaykhs.

Marriage is intended to be permanent, but divorce is not uncommon and carries no disgrace. Interfamily pressures act as a fairly strong deterrent to divorce, however, since husband and wife are usually closely related and their families will attempt to reconcile a couple's differences when they contemplate divorce. The most usual causes are incompatibility, barrenness, and lack of support. The procedure for the husband is very simple and requires only a declaration in the presence of two male witnesses of unimpeachable character of his intention to divorce his wife. He is expected to provide a short period of support for her and to take care of his young children, who generally stay with their mother until age twelve.

Women have more difficulty in obtaining a divorce, and pressure from families to carry on is considerably greater, but a woman can seek an end to her marriage through the office of a qadi. She must produce witnesses to substantiate her allegations, however—not always easy to do. Mistreatment, lack of support, desertion, or failure to obtain her consent before taking another wife are sufficient grounds for ending a marriage.

Islamic law strictly regulates inheritance. Men receive double the share of women, because women receive substantial dowries when they marry and are supported by their husbands. Women have, however, always been legally entitled to own, inherit, and bequeath property in their own names, even after marriage—a right acquired only recently in many far more developed countries. As a result, Saudi Arabia has thousands of very wealthy women, and banks provide sections reserved exclusively for women where they can manage their holdings without male interference.

Status of Women

Family customs are, of course, changing in Saudi Arabia as the oil industry and government development plans open up new avenues for making a living and achieving status. Salaried jobs greatly decrease economic dependence on family ties, and modern education transforms aspirations. The Saudi leadership has undertaken an ambitious program to provide education for all in the conviction that an educated citizenry can participate intelligently in its nation's affairs.

Schools for women, begun by the monarchy in 1959, were the initial impetus toward gradual change in the social status of women in the kingdom. The conscious goal of the government was to make women a stronger link in the chain of bonds which contribute to the cohesion of family and nation. The expansion in enrollments in the three ensuing decades has been phenomenal, and the impact cannot help but be far- reaching on the attitudes of Saudi women toward their roles both inside and outside the home. Saudi Arabia now has adequate schools for all girls who wish to attend, as well as colleges for women— and sections devoted to women in Saudi universities. Classes for women are staffed and run by women, unless male lecturers are brought in on closed-circuit television. A government which intends to suppress the female half of the population does not build schools for them.

The black *abbayah* which Saudi women wear over their clothes rivets the attention of Westerners, who are uncomfortable with the idea of hiding women from public view. Clothing habits reflect centuries of custom and have their origin in the heavy stress laid on family honor. Centuries ago the desert Bedouin might possess little besides his family name, which he came to value very highly. The greatest dishonor that could befall a man resulted from sexual misconduct by his daughter or sister (not his wife). Fathers and brothers (not her husband) must punish her to regain their honor. A husband took vengeance on his wife's lover for usurping his property rights.

This focus on family honor led to very strict codes to circumscribe sexual activity. Children learn all the sexual taboos at an early age and restrict their lives accordingly. In modern times rigid seclusion of women has prevailed among the urban middle classes and has status symbolism. In rural areas where women work in the fields or with the flocks, modesty prevails, but seclusion is impossible.

Hijab (Veil or Purdah)

Islam enjoins women to behave modestly in public, and the Qur'an mandates this manner. The custom of segregating the sexes acquired Islamic approval as a means of keeping women pure and out of reach of the baser appetites of society. The high value placed on personal honor led to this male preoccupation with female chastity. Conservative Saudi men believe they must control their women to uphold their honor.

O Prophet! Tell thy wives and daughters, and the believing women, that they should cast their outer garments over their persons (when abroad): That is most convenient that they should be known (as such) and not molested. God is Oft-Forgiving, Most Merciful.

Qur'an: XXXIII, 59

Say to the believing men that they should lower their gaze and guard their modesty: that will make for greater purity for them: And God is well acquainted with all that they do.

And say to the believing women that they should lower their gaze and guard their modesty; that they should not display their beauty and ornaments except what (must ordinarily) appear thereof; that they should draw their veils over their bosoms and not display their beauty except to their husbands, their father, their husbands' fathers, their sons, their husbands' sons, their brothers or their brothers' sons, or their sisters' sons, or their women, or the slaves whom their right hands possess, or male servants free of physical needs, or small children who have no sense of the shame of sex; and that they should not strike their feet in order to draw attention to their hidden ornaments.

And O ye Believers! Turn ye all together toward God, that ye may attain Bliss.

Qur'an: XXIV, 30-1

Islamic scholars differ on how the above scripture is to be interpreted. Some include women's hair in the category of 'adornment,' but not a woman's face. Others, including the Saudis, insist that female faces be covered. This Sura in the Quran also provided the religious impetus for the segregation of women from those men not included in the list of exempted kin relations. Although the Prophet Muhammad required his later wives to veil and avoid public contact with unrelated men, his first wife Khadija did not veil and reportedly was a participant in all of his meetings until her death in 619. The burden of contemporary interpretation of this stricture is thus left to the ulama.

The above verses were revealed at a time when pagan women dressed provocatively and codes of moral behavior were lax. The new rules were meant to improve social conditions for women without, however, weakening the reliance on masculine physical strength needed to cope with a primitive and demanding environment. Islam introduced such measures as the abolition of infanticide, limitation of polygamy, protection of widows and orphans, the marriage contract, and provision of dowry and inheritance rights for women—significant social reforms in the 7th century.

The fact that Saudi women wear the abbayah gives the impression that they are all in strict seclusion, completely cut off from contact with any men other than the members of their extended families. This may be the case with certain traditional families, but among families who have become involved in the activities of the outside world, many women, although they still wear their abbayahs on the street, mix socially with their husbands' friends, business associates, and casual acquaintances. The first generation of educated Saudi women, particularly those with university degrees, is finding its way in society. With their husbands' approval, they are welcoming in their homes a wide variety of male acquaintances whom they would not have been able to meet twenty-five years ago. These women are as poised, outgoing, and stimulating as educated women anywhere in the world.

The fact that there are thousands of Saudi female university professors, doctors, teachers and engineers proves that Saudi women were capable of performing in any profession. In the past, women were tutored at home and engaged in activities like teaching and nursing where they dealt only with other women, but in fields like these two the example of many non-veiled women from other Arab countries who have migrated to Saudi Arabia to meet job demands encouraged local women to expand the circle of their own activities.

If you ask a young Saudi woman with a university degree and a career of her own why she still wears the abbayah, she will tell you that in a society where women have been veiled for centuries, many of the men automatically assume that an unveiled woman is somehow immoral, and some will view her as a target for harassment. Wearing the abbayah avoids unpleasant incidents on the street, provoked by cheeky young men or by the public morality committees. The other side of the coin is that a woman who conforms to Saudi custom is protected in Saudi Arabia. No one is going to attack her or do her physical harm, for the men in her family will protect her with their lives.

Saudis explain that these things may change very gradually, and that gradual evolution of social customs over time is their goal, avoiding the destabilizing elements of revolutionary change. That evolution will require substantial changes in the habits and attitudes of men as well as women. For example, Arab men do not line up for service as Westerners do. At a reception desk or an airline counter where a group of men are competing for the clerk's attention, an unescorted woman would be completely ignored. Male taxi drivers will hesitate to pick up an unaccompanied woman in Saudi Arabia.

Deeply ingrained habits do not change overnight, or even within a generation. Practices as basic as child rearing contribute to these habits. Girls are taught as toddlers to be subordinate to the men in their lives. The men will argue that, because men perform public services for their wives and daughters, women do not need to appear in public. A whole new range of male outlooks must evolve if women are to move about comfortably in Saudi Arabia.

Restrictions on women keep half the population of Saudi Arabia from workplaces where men are employed. Women must have their father's or husband's support to enter the work force—support that requires a secure and sympathetic male. Critical manpower shortages, combined with increasing education opportunities for women, will help the change. In 1975 only 27,000 Saudi women were in the labor force. A decade later their numbers had increased to 120,000, with another 50,000 expected to join the work force by 1990.

These women obviously have male support in moving into the many aspects of education, into medicine and nursing, into the wide variety of social services now provided for women and children. Others find jobs as computer specialists, in bank sections exclusively for women (begun in 1980), running shops for women clientèle, as unseen voices in government radio and television, and as managers of women's personnel matters in the civil service. In 1983 the Institute of Public Administration started a separate training facility to prepare women for positions in the public sector.

Whoever works righteousness, man or woman, and has Faith, Verily, to him will We give a new Life, a life that is good and pure, and We will bestow on such their reward according to the best of their actions.

Qur'an: XVI, 97

When asked why they work, Saudi women seldom cite economic needs, for their standard of living is high. Rather, they mention altruism, personal fulfillment, and escape from the boredom of idleness. Those who work also cite their need for continuing education in new skills, for child care facilities, transportation, flexible work schedules, and a larger role in planning and decisionmaking—needs also expressed by women in the West.

The women of Saudi Arabia do not expect customs so deeply established to be abandoned quickly or abolished by government because the effect of rapid change would be too unsettling. Nor do Saudi women necessarily want to give up the security and services that their men now provide them. But the change in the status of women within the last sixty years is remarkable. Schools for girls were begun only in the 1960s, and met fierce opposition. Once King Faisal had education for women well established, he then reassured the religious scholars by making them the supervisory authority and permitted the introduction of many religious courses into the curriculum.

Restrictions have been reduced in other minor areas. A royal decree ordered that every Saudi woman have her photo in her passport, a completely new practice. Some women desire to be allowed to drive in Saudi Arabia. (Bedouin women drive their family's pickup trucks out in the country.) No law states that women can't drive, but a customary ban is strictly enforced in the cities. Actually, a woman in Saudi Arabia does not need to drive. Every family that can afford a car can pay some man, distantly related or otherwise, not trained for other employment who will happily drive the family automobile for a small salary.

The desire of Saudi women to drive is a matter of expanding their freedom of movement. In the fall of 1990, during the Gulf War, more than forty women, having obtained permission from their husbands or close male relatives, dismissed their chauffeurs and drove their cars through the streets of Riyadh. They were detained by police and their passports revoked. Six of them were suspended from their teaching positions at King Saud University in Riyadh. The Interior Minister announced a ban on all protests and demonstrations. A year later, King Fahd ordered their passports returned and the women compensated for any lost income resulting from their punishment.

The Political and Economic Ramifications of Family Connections

Because of a strong tradition of mutual obligations among families, business arrangements are apt to be organized on a family basis as well. Urban business concerns generally include a father, sons and brothers, or uncles and nephews working together. Nomadic encampments and farming villages are generally self-sustaining economic units, with land grazed or tilled in common by a large family unit. Every individual is expected to give assistance to related family members whenever the opportunity arises. Younger people are expected to take care of their elders and to enjoy doing so. This kind of ingroup support may not always be efficient, but it does provide all family members with a large degree of security.

The prominent tribes and clans do compete with each other in Saudi Arabia. Regional differences of opinion also exist, particularly between the outward-looking Hijazis and the more conservative tribes of the Najd, from which the ruling family derives. The Shiite population of the Eastern Province has at times chafed under government control, particularly in the 1970s when their province was the source of Saudi Arabia's huge wealth, but the revenues were spent all over the kingdom. Because the Arabian-American Oil Company provided good jobs and educational opportunities, a middle class of Shiite intelligentsia has emerged, which the government recognized after 1979, and the events in Iran. The government has instituted development projects in the Eastern Province to win more enthusiastic support there.

LANGUAGE AS A MAJOR FACTOR IN SAUDI CULTURE

Language shapes our perceptions and defines our concepts of time, space, distance, and the like. Because Arabic is an extraordinarily powerful medium of expression, its role is central in the culture of the Arab world.

No one knows how long the Arabic language has been spoken, but the Arabian Peninsula is certainly its homeland. The remarkable aspect of its origin is that Arabic evolved very early into a splendid poetic idiom among a nomadic pastoral people who were both illiterate and sparsely dispersed over an enormous geographical region. The Bedouin poet was the repository of his tribe's history and genealogy. Because the Peninsula Arabs were nomadic, language was perhaps all they had to utilize for intellectual stimulation and entertainment. In any case, long before the birth of the Prophet Muhammad, Arabic tribal poetry had developed a wealth of vocabulary, several distinct meters, and an opulent imagery that were the fountainhead of classical Arabic.

In the Prophet's time the poet was the historian and spokesman of his tribe. Because he knew the tribal lore and traditions, and expressed in his poetry the ideals of gallantry, courage, loyalty, independence, honesty, and generosity, he had the power to both inspire and sustain his people.

This heritage, imbedded in the Quran, was diffused throughout the world by the spread of Islam. Written Arabic was not common before Muhammad's time, but the inspired style of the Quran has provided the model for all subsequent Arabic literature. Much of the Quran's impact when it is chanted (as it was meant to be), lies in the cadence and rhetoric of the language, which is lost when it is translated out of Arabic. The style is sonorous and rhythmic, an expression of the rhymed prose of traditional Arabic tribal poetry.

Beginning in the 7th century, the Arabs of the Arabian Peninsula carried their language to all their neighbors, who originally spoke Semitic languages. It replaced Aramaic, spoken across the Fertile Crescent, and Coptic, spoken in Egypt—defining the borders of what is known today as the Arab world. It did not supplant Persian in Iran, Pushtu in Afghanistan, Kurdish in Kurdistan, Turkish in Turkey, or Turkic in Central Asia, although Muslims in all those areas became familiar with the language of the Quran.

The empire did not endure, but the Arabic language is spoken today by about 215 million people spread over 4.5 million square miles of the Middle East and Africa. Its alphabet is second only to the Latin alphabet in the extent of its usage. Even in countries with local languages completely different from Arabic, the scriptures of the religion, contained in the Quran and the sayings of the Prophet Muhammad, are learned in Arabic (whether understood or not) wherever Islam is practiced. The one-fifth of the human race which professes the Muslim religion venerates Arabic as a language of special power and elegance.

For the Arabians themselves, their language has a strong emotional appeal which touches and moves them in much the same way music does. At family celebrations and at gatherings during religious holidays, trained reciters read Quranic passages and formal, traditional poems describing the life of the Prophet, which are received with rapt attention. Such readings are common on the radio. Indeed, King

Abdul Aziz justified the introduction of radio in Makkah (Mecca) in the 1920s as a vehicle for widespread transmission of the Quran. Arabs generally admire individuals who can recite from memory long sections of the Quran, and memorizing it was the major activity of the traditional religious schools.

Professional bards are still popular everywhere, especially during Ramadan, the month of fasting. They compose and sing poems for wedding feasts and other rites of passage, and new epics are produced for the installation of a king or important shaykh, or to mark his passing. Laborers sing work songs while winnowing grain, pitting dates, riding camels, herding goats, loading cargo, trimming sail on ships, even while driving bulldozers or manning oil rigs. Many casual singers accompany themselves, either on traditional lute, drum, tambourine, or one-string fiddle, or with that versatile adaptation from the New World which has a name of Arab origin—the guitar.

Spoken Arabic includes a number of separate and distinct regional dialects, not always understood from region to region, but the written language known as classical Arabic—the polished language of the Quran—is used universally by all literate Arabic-speaking peoples. The ability to speak in formal Arabic is considered a mark of erudition, not shared by or even comprehended by the ordinary citizen.

The exceptionally high value that Arabs put on their language causes them to overassert, to exaggerate, and to repeat far more than English speakers. In Arabic the words for "eloquence" and "exaggeration" come from the same verbal root. Their love of drama, mystery, romance, poetry, and imagination blurs mundane distinctions between fact and fiction. This leads to confusion when foreigners take what Arabs say at face value, while Arabs are not convinced of the validity of simple assertions in English.

Arabs often use verbal threats to relieve tension, substituting words for action and giving psychological relief to the speaker. (Saddam Hussein's boasting during the Gulf War was an extreme example.) The power of Arabic rhetoric also leads the Arabs to assert verbal actions of wish fulfillment that enhance their pride without any reality to back them up. (Saddam Hussein assured the Iraqis that they had won the Gulf War.) Non-Arabs have a tendency to interpret translations of speeches by Arab leaders literally, without understanding how much exaggeration is imbedded in the language.

Another source of great confusion for Westerners in understanding Arabs is that Arabic verb tenses do not correspond to ours. Arabic has no future tense, while the same imperfect verb form expresses several different tenses, including the future. Language defines experience for its speakers. Unlike English, where verb tenses define and organize the flow of events, Arabic verbs are somewhat vague, and do not focus on historical sequence. People using such a verb structure do not have a rigid sequential sense of time. The Arab's sense of history is not stretched out on a time line; rather, it is focused on the occurrence of clusters of important events. The tendency to overstate any case to the point where it seems exaggerated to non-Arabs, combined with the lack of precision as to the relationship of specific events to the other activities that are part of man's behavior, leads to misunderstandings and communication gaps between Arabs and non-Arabs.

THE ARABIC LANGUAGE

Arabic is a Semitic language, one of a group of ancient languages of which only Arabic is widely spoken today. Arabic is written from right to left on the page in an artistically flowing cursive script. The Arabic alphabet, developed originally and streamlined by the Phoenicians, has twenty-eight letters, all representing consonants. Vowels are indicated by marks above and below the letters, although these are ordinarily omitted.

The transliteration of Arabic into English is difficult because the Arabic alphabet contains letters which the English does not, as well as sounds for which there are no English equivalents. The letter 'ain, for example, is usually represented by ' and signifies a minute pause with a catch in the breath. The word Saudi, for example, should have an 'ain between the a and the u, so that it is spoken in three syllables.

Arabic names of places and people often seem very confusing, but much of this difficulty arises from the transliteration of Arabic words into the English alphabet. The Red Sea port of Jiddah, for example, is also commonly spelled Jeddah and Juddah. The problem rests in English spellings, not with Arabic.

In Arabic, as in French, all nouns have gender, and the article "the" (al) precedes them. A number of common English words which have come directly from Arabic retain the al: albatross, alcohol, alfalfa, algebra, algorithm, alchemy, almanac, and alkali are examples.

Other common English words derived from Arabic are atlas (atlas), banana (banan), camel (jamal), cotton (qutun), gazelle ghazal), lemon (limun), magazine (makhazin), safari (safariy), sugar (sukkar), syrup (sharab), and cipher (sifr).

Dinner feast among friends in Najran.

Bedouin women braiding a young girl's hair.

Man sitting with incense.

At Madain Saleh in northwest Saudi Arabia, the
Nabataeans established an important trade center.

Handicrafts in Al Junadriyah.

Chapter 5
PETROLEUM AND THE SAUDI ECONOMY

One out of every four barrels of oil produced in the world today comes from Saudi Arabia. In the last twenty years, the Saudi treasury has been enriched by approximately $800 billion in oil revenues. The kingdom's proven reserves are estimated at 315 billion barrels—the largest in the world, sufficient to maintain current production levels for well over a century. Because of these huge petroleum reserves, Saudi Arabia plays a vital role in world economics.

PETROLEUM TRANSFORMS SAUDI ARABIA

Several American oil companies were searching for oil abroad in the 1920s. Standard Oil of California (SOCAL) chartered the Bahrain Petroleum Company, Ltd., in Canada in 1930, and discovered oil in Bahrain two years later. Having established a good reputation, SOCAL then negotiated an agreement with King Abdul Aziz Ibn Saud to explore the east coast region of Saudi Arabia—just twenty miles away from Bahrain Island. SOCAL formed the California Arabian Standard Oil Company (CASOC) to exploit the concession.

The Origins of the Arabian-American Oil Company

The first geologists came by boat from Bahrain and used camels to transport their equipment to their first camp in the coastal village called Dammam. A handful of men attempted to pinpoint the best spots to drill for oil in a concession that covered 320,000 square miles. An airplane finally arrived from the States to do aerial observations and photographs needed for more detailed geological studies. After two years' surface examination of the terrain, these first prospectors decided that the Dammam Dome was the spot to test.

Next came engineers, construction men, and drillers, who must be housed and supplied with both equipment and food, none of which was available in eastern Arabia. The small fishing village of Al Khobar was selected as the site for a long rock pier, built by Saudi work crews, where small boats and barges could unload imported supplies. A camp was constructed at Dhahran to house the workmen. Seven test holes were drilled between 1934 and 1937 without finding oil in commercial quantities. The seventh hole was about to be abandoned when the hunch of one of the wildcatters led them to go deeper—to almost five thousand feet. Liquid gold gushed out of the sand.

Finding the oil was only the first step in a lengthy and complex process. A storage and shipping terminal had to be constructed to ship the oil, and a pipeline to get it from the well to the port. The first oil was sent by barge to the Bahrain Petroleum Company refinery twenty-five miles away. In 1937 The Texas Company bought half ownership of CASOC, providing additional funds for expansion. If oil was to be shipped elsewhere, a facility to load tankers was needed. Ras Tanura was chosen for a marine terminal. A larger pipeline, storage tanks, pumps, moorings, and submarine loading lines were constructed to a deep-water anchorage over half a mile offshore. By 1939 a large stabilizer plant was completed in Dhahran to remove poisonous hydrogen sulfide gas before the crude oil could be shipped.

A community had to be built to house the much larger work staff which would be involved in producing oil for export. In Dhahran dormitories, cottages, and apartments were erected for the crews and their families. Located in the open desert, the community required a dining hall, clubhouse, and swimming pool for recreation, a commissary for shopping, storehouses for supplies, a central air-conditioning plant to make life bearable in the desert heat.

Shipping difficulties, tanker shortages, and inaccessibility of markets during World War II slowed operations considerably. Only a skeleton staff remained in Dhahran to supply crude oil to the Bahrain refinery. The employees who remained behind kept busy. They surveyed the water resources in the Al Kharj region southeast of Riyadh, permitting the reclamation and irrigation of an extensive tract for agriculture. They kept their scant fleet of vehicles running with whatever parts they could rig up, and used them to haul emergency food when a severe drought threatened the Saudis. They fattened their own sheep and cattle for food, turned one of their air-conditioned cottages into a brooder for hatching chickens, and grew their own vegetables.

By 1943 the Allied war effort was requiring enormous quantities of oil, and the United States government allocated materials to construct a refinery at Ras Tanura, plus the needed trucks and construction equipment. The project included storage tanks, loading lines, a T-shaped pier with large tanker berths, and a submarine pipeline to the Bahrain refinery, which was being enlarged. The quiet holding operation in Dhahran turned almost overnight into pandemonium, as men struggled to cope with both the complications of a large construction project far from its supplies and the confusion of getting scarce items in wartime.

The refinery went into operation in 1945, and by the end of that year the newly-renamed Arabian-American Oil Company (ARAMCO) had discovered two more oilfields. In 1946 Standard Oil Company (New Jersey—now Exxon) and Socony-Vacuum Oil Company (now Mobile Oil Corporation) joined CASOC and The Texas Company as part owners of ARAMCO. With the end of the war, production was rapidly increased. In 1951 ARAMCO discovered its first offshore reservoir 150 miles north of Dhahran; called Safaniya, it is one of the largest in the world. Important new discoveries followed in the later 1950s. In 1951 the Saudi government paid ARAMCO to build a railroad from Dammam south to Riyadh. By 1974, 300 wells were operating in sixteen different fields, with all the required equipment, support services, crews, pipelines, and the rest.

The Petroleum Industry as a Development Model

Efficient production of oil in large quantities depends on three crucial factors—infrastructure (utilities, transportation, communications, and the rest), human resources, and support services. Because Saudi Arabia was a desert economy dependent on agriculture and commerce, ARAMCO's task was to put in place all the basic necessities for the oil industry.

All kinds of additional facilities were needed— enlarged marine terminals, including a tanker-loading sea island; more storage tanks; more stabilization plants; a greatly expanded electric power grid.

Enlarged and more efficient refinery capacity was provided at Ras Tanura to process crude oil into the components for consumer products—naphtha and light gases, kerosene, gasoline, light and heavy diesel oils, fuel oils, jet fuel, and asphalt. New processes were begun, such as the production and export of natural gas liquids (propane, butane, and natural gas). Computers were introduced to study reservoir conditions requiring gas and liquid injection programs, and to work out decisions as to where and when to drill wells. Gas injection plants were built to return compressed gas into oil-bearing formations so that natural energy would force oil to the surface without pumping.

Geologists ventured into the Empty Quarter, using helicopters, air-conditioned trailers, sand buggies with oversize pressure tires, and truck convoys to supply camps in the trackless desert. In addition to hunting for oil, the geologists helped the government produce maps of all of Saudi Arabia. To simplify the shipping of oil to Europe, ARAMCO's owner company built a 754-mile pipeline from the oil fields to Sidon on the Mediterranean coast in Lebanon. The construction of the Trans-Arabian Pipeline (Tapline) involved complex logistics in moving men and supplies across a rugged, largely deserted terrain, where roads, camps, water, food, and transport all had to be brought in. Finished in 1950, Tapline had complete communities to man the five pump stations, with repair shops, supply depots, airstrips, communications, housing, hospitals, schools, feeding and recreation facilities, utilities, offices, and roads. These facilities attracted settlers so that the pump stations became centers of flourishing towns. The completion of Tapline substantially increased revenues flowing into the kingdom.

Involving the Saudis in the Petroleum Industry

Facilities were only half the picture, however. Producing, refining, and shipping oil, plus all the support services involved, required a wide range of human resources. In a region like Eastern Arabia, inhabited by oasis farmers and nomadic herdsmen, the only way to utilize local manpower was to train it and to provide the needed social services. ARAMCO provided good jobs and an education to large numbers of residents of the Eastern Province where the oil fields are located. These opportunities were particularly appreciated by the Shiite Muslims, who make up the majority of the population in the area.

In the beginning training was informal, on-the-job teaching of drillers, craftsmen, office workers. Soon academic and craftshop classroom programs were added. Later the company began paying for employee education or advanced vocational training overseas. Industrial Training Centers were established at Abqaiq, Dhahran, Ras Tanura, Dammam, and Al Hasa, to give instruction in Arabic, English, Math, the sciences, Social Studies, and in the operation of business machines. By 1975 more than fifty-five hundred Saudi employees were enrolled.

The services needed by the growing cadre of Saudi employees moved ARAMCO to encourage other businesses. The Arab Industrial Development Department of ARAMCO resulted, with the company providing financial or technical assistance to local enterprises to do everything from growing vegetables for local markets to making the bags the vegetables are carried in, trucking produce and supplies from source to customer, running bus companies, printing presses, electric companies, construction companies, water drilling companies, dairies, cement plants, hatcheries, and all the rest.

These amicable and constructive activities undertaken by the Arabian-American Oil Company in its first thirty years of operation provided an on-site case study of how infrastructure, human resources, and support services must be integrated into the development process. This large-scale model was operating successfully on Saudi soil when the Saudi rulers undertook the massive development of the whole country in the 1970s. ARAMCO's careful attention to the needs and welfare of all those involved in the oil industry contributed to a favorable reception by the Saudis of American attitudes and technology.

Creation of Wealth for the Saudis

The transformation of formerly barren desert areas into bustling modern complexes, crisscrossed with highways, pipelines, and utility grids, and dotted with modern towns and ports, is not the only legacy of the oil industry. In all the Arab countries, underground oil is the property of the state. The royalties paid by oil companies for exploration rights and profits from sales of crude oil that accrue to the local government have provided the revenue to transform the rest of the country.

Once oil in commercial quantities was found, the usual practice of oil companies before 1970 was to allocate a fixed percentage of their revenues as payment to the local state treasury. In Saudi Arabia that share went directly to King Abdul Aziz. In 1950 the concession agreement was revised to provide a fifty-fifty split of profits with the monarch, although oil company manipulation of tax laws made that split less generous than it sounded.

TABLE 6
SAUDI ARABIA OIL PRODUCTION AND VALUE OF EXPORTS

Year	Production	Value
1938	1,357 bpd	Not available
1939	10,778 bpd	N.A.
1940	13,866 bpd	N.A.
1941	11,809 bpd	N.A.
1942	12,412 bpd	N.A.
1943	13,337 bpd	N.A.
1944	21,296 bpd	N.A.
1945	58,386 bpd	N.A.
1946	164,229 bpd	N.A.
1947	246,169 bpd	N.A.
1948	390,309 bpd	N.A.
1949	476,736 bpd	N.A.
1950	546,703 bpd	N.A.
1951	761,541 bpd	N.A.
1952	824,757 bpd	N.A.
1953	844,642 bpd	N.A.
1954	953,000 bpd	N.A.
1955	965,041 bpd	N.A.
1956	986,129 bpd	N.A.
1957	992,114 bpd	N.A.
1958	1,015,029 bpd	US$ 786,133,330
1959	1,095,399 bpd	884,400,000
1960	1,247,140 bpd	1,036,933,300
1961	1,392,518 bpd	1,128,293,300
1962	1,520,703 bpd	1,135,120,000
1963	1,629,018 bpd	1,418,186,700
1964	1,716,105 bpd	1,595,840,000
1965	2,024,870 bpd	1,823,660,000
1966	2,392,737 bpd	2,030,480,000
1967	2,597,563 bpd	2,094,026,700
1968	2,829,982 bpd	2,473,013,300
1969	2,992,662 bpd	N.A.

1970	3,548,865 bpd	2,418,000,000
1971	4,497,576 bpd	3,803,000,000
1972	5,733,395 bpd	5,477,000,000
1973	7,334,647 bpd	8,956,000,000
1974	8,209,706 bpd	35,476,000,000
1975	6,826,942 bpd	29,473,000,000
1976	8,343,953 bpd	38,157,000,000
1977	9,016,952 bpd	43,308,000,000
1978	8,066,105 bpd	41,332,000,000
1979	9,251,079 bpd	62,855,000,000
1980	9,631,366 bpd	105,813,000,000
1981	9,623,828 bpd	116,183,000,000
1982	6,327,220 bpd	75,534,000,000
1983	4,374,300 bpd	42,809,000,000
1984	3,922,079 bpd	34,243,000,000
1985	3,041,104 bpd	24,180,000,000
1986	4,689,800 bpd	16,975,000,000
1987	3,991,000 bpd	19,271,000,000
1988	4,928,100 bpd	19,607,000,000
1989	4,863,533 bpd	24,093,000,000
1990	6,257,600 bpd	39,700,000,000

*barrels per day
Source: OPEC, *Annual Statistical Bulletin*, 1990.
Saudi ARAMCO, *Annual Report*, 1990.

TABLE 7
MEMBERS OF OPEC AND DATES JOINED

Iran (founding member)	1960
Iraq (founding member)	1960
Kuwait (founding member)	1960
Saudi Arabia (founding member)	1960
Venezuela (founding member)	1960
Qatar	1960
Libya	1962
Indonesia	1962
United Arab Emirates	1967
Algeria	1969
Nigeria	1971
Ecuador (inactive status, 1992)	1973
Gabon (associate member)	1973

OPEC Enters the World Petroleum Picture

In 1960 five oil-producing countries (Iran, Venezuela, Saudi Arabia, Kuwait, and Iraq) formed the Organization of Petroleum Exporting Countries (OPEC) and succeeded in freezing the posted prices of crude oil at around $2 a barrel so that their share remained stable rather than fluctuating with changing market conditions. OPEC then began demanding that foreign oil companies accept their host government as full partners in the industry.

Political Crises Affect the Petroleum Industry

External events, particularly the 1967 Arab- Israeli War and the 1968 presidential election in the United States, had a major impact on the Middle East oil industry. A decade earlier the United States had forced Israel to withdraw from Suez, but Cold War politics changed United States policy in the Middle East. Rather than pressuring Israel to give up the territories she conquered in 1967, American aid to Israel was greatly increased to counter the arms being sent by the USSR to Syria and Egypt. The result was such an upsurge in Palestinian nationalism sponsored by the Palestine Liberation Organization (PLO) that King Hussain of Jordan felt compelled to forcibly drive Yasser Arafat and his forces from his kingdom in 1970. The Palestinian leaders, convinced of the righteousness of their cause, challenged all the entrenched Arab leaders to back them.

That wave of unrest spilled over into Saudi Arabia. Anti-American demonstrations broke out in Riyadh, Qatif, Dammam, Al Khobar, and Ras Tanura. Radical Palestinians set a bomb to the Saudi Tapline in the Golan Heights. Disenchanted students from the College of Petroleum and Minerals in Dhahran attacked ARAMCO installations, the airbase, and the United States consulate. The Saudi National Guard intervened to prevent serious bloodshed, and radical ringleaders of a small Saudi opposition were arrested to prevent further conspiracies.

The one bright spot was a new Egyptian leader, Anwar Sadat, with whom King Faisal was very comfortable. Following Saudi advice, Sadat expelled his Soviet advisers in 1972. Washington not only failed to respond, but another presidential election campaign brought increased support to Israel. King Faisal was so incensed that he laid down an ultimatum to the oil companies: Saudi participation in oil production should be implemented immediately. The oil company officials assumed he was bluffing.

In 1973 the Egyptian army crossed the Suez in an attempt to recapture the Sinai, while the Syrians marched on the Golan Heights. Saudi Arabia began the imposition of a gradual oil embargo, which unfortunately coincided with the Watergate affair in Washington. President Nixon, absorbed in the disintegration of his presidency, delegated the handling of the Middle East crisis to his Secretary of State, Henry Kissinger.

The 1973 Oil Embargo

Because the Soviets were airlifting supplies to Egypt and Syria, Kissinger saw the crisis in Cold War terms and began a massive counter-airlift to Israel. Nixon asked Congress to fund $2.2 billion in emergency aid (much of it already in the pipeline)—an amount far in excess of Israel's needs. King Faisal felt betrayed and responded by announcing a total oil embargo to countries aiding Israel. The other Arab members of OPEC, except for Libya and Iraq, followed suit. Production quickly dropped 60 to 70 percent, causing worldwide prices of crude oil to quadruple.

Several coincidences contributed to the new situation. By 1973 OPEC controlled 85 percent of the world's oil exports, at a time when the demand was increasing for greater and greater amounts of energy around the world. When demand exceeded supply, the seller could set the price. The shock effect of the quadrupling of oil prices might have been more effectively resisted by the oil importers had it not coincided with the 1973 Arab oil embargo against the countries which helped Israel against Egypt and Syria.

The cutoff of Arab oil forced the industrialized countries to face three stark facts: Their economies were so dependent on petroleum that they were forced to pay whatever price the market demanded. The non-Arab oil-producing nations could not supply their needs, so that a long-term embargo could prove disastrous to the economies of some countries, particularly Japan. And finally, the Arab oil embargo had coincided by accident with almost the exact moment in history when production of oil in the United States began to decline. Although the United States was not hit as hard by the embargo as Europe and Japan, she was no longer the world's leading oil producer. Saudi Arabian production almost equalled American in 1974, and Soviet oil production moved into first place in 1975.

For the Western world, the 1970s were a rude contrast to the previous decade. The Soviet Union had dumped its oil surpluses on the world market in the 1960s, contributing to a worldwide glut. Oil sold for less than $2 a barrel. Cheap oil had given the West an era of unprecedented prosperity and permitted a heedless indulgence in private automobiles, air conditioning, and gadgets/appliances of every sort. Oil costing $10 to $12 a barrel changed the whole economic equation.

It is important to realize that these events did not have a cause and effect relationship. The increasing energy shortages in industrialized countries, which resulted from continuous multiple rises in demand, were inevitable, with or without OPEC or the Arab oil embargo. OPEC members successfully raised oil prices because of the continually mounting demand for energy, and the oil embargo forced the industrial countries to face the dilemma resulting from increasing dependence on foreign oil.

An oil embargo is in no way illegal. Every country in the world is privileged to decide to whom it wishes to sell its products. Constraints on levels of production may be legitimate conservation measures, with producers preferring to stretch out production to fit their local capital needs, keeping prices high, rather than pumping oil to meet foreign demands.

The regulatory aspects of OPEC bothered some critics because the organization was fixing prices, but non-member producers like Canada followed OPEC in raising prices. The sensible way to combat high prices is to decrease demand so that the seller lowers his price. Only energy conservation and a search for alternate sources of energy could lower costs.

The 1973 oil embargo was a major turning point in modern Arab history. Losses to Israel on the battlefield were mitigated by the realization that petroleum producers had worldwide economic clout. After 1973 the king of Saudi Arabia was a force to be reckoned with—in a position to bargain from strength. European nations abandoned their neutrality and openly supported the Arab cause. The PLO won observer status at the UN, and a resolution was pushed through the General Assembly calling for a Palestinian homeland in the West Bank and Gaza Strip.

Although he was unable to accomplish all he wanted, King Faisal lifted the oil blockade in 1974. In return he received promises of American weapons and technology. The Joint Commission on Economic Cooperation between the two countries was initiated and the military aid program increased.

Technology was more important to the Saudis than arms, for they were now accumulating oil revenues faster than they could spend them. Two choices were open: Invest the excess revenue abroad where inflation would eat up the profits, or spend the money developing Saudi Arabia. King Faisal chose the latter course, but realized that he needed outside assistance to do so.

The Saudi oil minister negotiated an agreement to take over 25 percent ownership of ARAMCO's producing facilities and in 1974 upped that share to 60 percent. In 1980 the Saudi government took complete control of ARAMCO, with a contract arrangement for the foreign companies which became partners to continue certain activities such as refining and marketing on a concession basis. The name was changed to the Saudi Arabian Oil Company (Saudi Aramco).

PETROMIN

In 1962, the Saudis set up a special agency, the General Organization of Petroleum and Minerals (PETROMIN), to develop the entire natural resource sector of the kingdom. Such a local institution permitted different kinds of concessionary arrangements from those negotiated in the 1930s. Instead of leaving all the technical activities to foreign oil companies in return for a fixed percentage fee, the Saudis after 1974 made agreements for joint exploration, production, refining, and marketing, with contracts stipulating that substantial investments will be made by the foreign company, either as a bonus payment to the Saudi government or in the form of large exploration outlays. (All or part of these initial expenses could be recovered by the foreign company if commercial production of oil was realized.)

At the same time, PETROMIN gave priority to encouraging Saudi private investment and the expansion of job opportunities for Saudis by the establishment of new industries using Saudi Arabia's natural resources. PETROMIN has entered into agreements with foreign firms for the joint production of a wide range of petrochemicals, such as ammonia, urea, and plastics.

Today PETROMIN deals only with the distribution and marketing of petroleum products within the kingdom. As the kingdom's oil industry is restructured, Petromin is expected to become a state holding company, with shares in all of the specialized oil company subsidiaries.

SAMAREC

In 1993 SAMAREC was merged into ARAMCO to centralize relations connected to the oil industries.

The World Petroleum Industry in the 1980s

The Iranian revolution in 1979 severely disrupted Iranian oil production. Crude oil prices shot from $13 to $28 a barrel. The Western nations, already struggling with economic recession, turned to conservation and investment in alternative sources of energy. World consumption of petroleum dropped 4.7 percent. The Saudis immediately grasped the importance of keeping a lid on prices and upped their production to encourage consumption, a policy they have followed ever since.

Saudi policy, adopted in spite of differences of opinion among Saudi policymakers, was to produce the optimum amount of oil to moderate prices and protect the Western economies where Saudi surplus revenues were invested. They have repeatedly increased or decreased their level of production over the last two decades to maintain a stable price level—often in the face of gross cheating by other OPEC members on their quotas. Some of the Saudis would have opted for conservation of oil resources, slower economic growth, and less social disruption. Those opposing this viewpoint, argued that slower rates of production and high prices would drive consumers toward alternate sources of energy. They felt that political stability in Saudi Arabia required oil prices at a level that would not drastically decrease national income.

In 1980 the Iran-Iraq War again disrupted oil production, and the Saudis took up the slack, forcing other countries to hold the line on price increases. Overproduction by other OPEC countries soon led to an oil glut. Saudi Arabia, attempting to maintain stable oil prices, cut production. Its share of OPEC oil exports fell from nearly 43 percent in 1981 to just over 21 percent in 1985—with a devastating effect on the Saudi economy and development plans. In order to pressure other oil producers to cooperate in working for a stable market, Saudi Arabia decided in 1985 to produce its full quota, regardless of the effect. Prices fell to $10 a barrel, closing down North American facilities that couldn't produce oil economically at that price. The following year OPEC members agreed, after pressure from the United States, to reduce production to achieve an $18-dollar-a-barrel price level. Oil prices began to recover by the end of the year.

The Gulf War Disrupts the Middle East

The struggle to maintain that level continued until Iraq's invasion of Kuwait in 1990. The volatility in oil prices was very well illustrated in the first weeks of Desert Storm: With Iraq's invasion of Kuwait, crude oil prices rose immediately to above $28 a barrel. When allied air attacks began against Iraq in 1991, crude oil prices rose to $35 a barrel. They fell slightly when American troops headed for Saudi Arabia.

By October crude oil prices reached $40.42 a barrel—a new record. Saudi Arabia raised its production from 5.5 million barrels per day (bpd) to almost 8.5 million bpd to bring prices back down to normal levels. Non-Arab countries also increased their production to make up the shortfall of lost Kuwaiti and Iraqi oil. Reports of successful air attacks against Iraq caused prices to fall to $17.91, prompting OPEC ministers to meet to assess the situation. Speculation that OPEC would cut production levels pushed prices back up.

Quotas were obviously not observed, because by February 1992 OPEC oil production had reached an 11- year high of 24.2 million bpd, priced at approximately $16 a barrel. Kuwait's production was coming back on line, contributing to the glut. In June 1992 (after Desert Storm), OPEC voted to maintain a 22.3 million bpd production ceiling, aiming at a $21-a-barrel benchmark price. That level was obviously exceeded, for in February 1993 OPEC ministers agreed to reduce production to 23.6 million bpd in order to boost prices. Rivalries among the producers will determine whether the latest quotas are observed.

Saudi Arabia has the capacity to pump ten million barrels of oil per day. Continuing exploration has revealed new fields, with the kingdom's reserves estimated at roughly 25 percent of the world's total—enough for 150 years of production at 1987 levels. Gas reserves are estimated at 177.3 trillion cubic feet.

The present Saudi policy is to keep oil priced moderately. Rising prices would cause a surge in new non-OPEC oil production, efforts to achieve greater efficiency in use of oil, or substitution of other energy sources. Saudi Minister of Petroleum and Mineral Resources Hisham M. Nazer recently explained Saudi policy: The goal is to maintain "prices that assure a reasonable return to the producer and predictability to the consumer. We also believe there is a mutual bond of self-interest between ourselves and our major oil customers. By meeting the needs of our customers with a steady flow of oil at stable prices, we turn our geological endowment into the hard currency that has financed our economic development. In return, the customer provides us with access to his market, and his economy enjoys the benefits of oil at reasonable prices." (Speech at Harvard Business School, May 1992)

Changes in World Petroleum Production

The world petroleum situation is affected very much by the fact that oil is an exhaustible resource, and political events affect petroleum production. Kuwait's oil production was halted by the Iraqi invasion and the firing of the wellheads by retreating Iraqi troops. Two years of repair work were needed before Kuwaiti production began to come back on line. Iraq has not been exporting oil since 1990 because Saddam Hussein will not permit the UN to control oil income for humanitarian purposes and reparations.

Russia, briefly the world's largest producer, has seen her petroleum production fall drastically and cannot expect it to rise until large investments are made in modern extraction techniques and improved distribution. Russia produced 10.2 million bpd in 1991, but that level is expected to drop to 9.2 million bpd by end of 1992 and to 8.7 million bpd in 1993.

American oil output has decreased steadily since the 1970s, and many American wells are no longer profitable. United States production in 1992 was at 7 million bpd and dropping as old fields dry up and are not replaced. This level meets barely half of domestic demand (16.5 million bpd in 1991, which was 3 percent lower than in 1990). Demand is expected to remain flat in the United States over the next few years.

ECONOMIC AND SOCIAL DEVELOPMENT
IN SAUDI ARABIA

When King Abdul Aziz Ibn Saud passed away in 1953, Saudi Arabia was heavily in debt. His generosity had led to borrowing against future oil revenues. His son King Saud embarked on a huge construction program—schools, highways, government buildings—while continuing the large entourage he had inherited from his father. In 1958 the kingdom was on the brink of bankruptcy.

When Crown Prince Faisal was put in charge, he immediately set to work balancing Saudi Arabia's budget—for the first time in history. He separated royal from public expenditure in the national accounts, and capped the generous stipends of royal family members.

In Saudi Arabia the government administration created by the monarch has monopolistic power over the distribution of economic resources. King Faisal decided that the bureaucracy's decisive role in the economic system had to be regularized in order to efficiently allocate public benefits among various social and geographical divisions in the country. Government should also provide a wide range of incentives to help private businesses deemed to be in the public interest. Over the years there has been a positive correlation between the growth of government revenue and expansion of bureaucratic functions.

Development Planning

After Faisal became king in 1964, the tremendous growth in oil wealth made it obvious that Saudi Arabia could not continue to spend its revenues in a random fashion. In 1970 he set up a planning office and instituted a series of five-year development plans. The first program, modest in nature, committed $11 billion to developing basic infrastructure and improving government services in urban areas—particularly education, social services, transportation, and communications. Water supply systems received close attention, with desalinization plants built at Jiddah, Khobar, and Khafji, and smaller ones begun at Um Luj and Jubail. The goal was to introduce some of the benefits of modernization and higher standards of living without sacrificing traditional social and moral values.

In 1975 the Central Planning Organization was elevated to ministry status, and the focus of planning shifted from expanding current amenities to assessment of the kingdom's future needs. That year Saudi Arabia lost the far-sighted king who had begun the coherent planning, but his successors, King Khalid and King Fahd, carried on what had been set in motion.

King Khalid (1975-1982) was a much more old-fashioned father figure than Faisal—generous, pious, dutiful, who loved falconry and camping in the desert with the Bedouin. The brother who assisted him, Crown Prince Fahd, was urbane, sophisticated, and an ardent administrator who kept the modernization process in control. When Fahd became king in 1982, he understood the challenges both the kingdom and his family faced. The government's task in spending the cash coming into Saudi Arabia was to promote national stability.

The second plan (1975-80) outlined expenditures of $139 billion, much of it for new construction around the kingdom to complete the needed infrastructure and diversify the economic base. The results were impressive: the length of paved highways tripled, power generation increased 28 times, capacity of seaports grew tenfold. The nonoil sector showed steady growth and accounted for 24.2 percent of government revenue in 1983. There were sharp increases in the production of cement, chemical fertilizers, and many agricultural crops.

But oil production tumbled after 1981 when world demand for oil declined. The drop in Saudi production (mentioned earlier) from a high of almost 10 million bpd to a little over 3 million bpd by 1985 was felt in all sectors of the economy, but particularly in petrochemicals where Saudi prices, which reflected expensive foreign labor and technology and the high price of desalinated water, were not competitive on the world market.

Early in 1985 work was stopped on two refineries, even though orders were already taken and engineering work nearly complete. The Saudis were forced to do some shrewd bargaining to assure markets, linking sales of crude oil overseas to the purchase of refined products from Saudi Arabia.

Government cut back spending by 20 percent in 1984 to balance the budget. Saudi Arabia weathered the drop in oil revenues by drawing on its foreign reserves. Retrenchment had certain advantages, such as the easing of economic and social strains. Money was spent more carefully. The need for an ever-growing number of foreign workers decreased. University standards were tightened, improving the quality of education, although graduates found it more difficult to find employment.

TABLE 8
GOVERNMENT REVENUES AND EXPENDITURE
(in millions of Riyals)

Year	Revenues	Expenditure	Balance
1973/74	98,247	45,743	52,504
1974/75	95,847	110,935	-15,088
1975/76	110,935	131,296	-20,318
1976/77	146,493	134,253	12,240
1977/78	130,000	144,558	-14,558
1978/79	160,000	185,820	-25,820
1979/80	261,516	245,000	16,516
1980/81	340,000	298,000	42,000
1981/82	313,000	313,000	000
1982/83	225,000	260,000	-35,000
1983/84	214,000	260,000	-46,000
1984/85	200,000	200,000	000
1985/86	200,000	200,000	000
1986/87	117,380	170,000	-52,620
1987/88	105,300	141,200	-35,900
1988/89	N.A.	140,459	N.A.
1989/90	118,000	143,000	-25,000
1991/92	118,000	143,000	-25,000

Source: Ministry of Finance and National Economy, *Statistical Yearbook*, Kingdom of Saudi Arabia, 1991.

Decreasing Saudi Reliance on Crude Oil Resources

The Fourth Development Plan, released in the spring of 1985, contained a sobering recognition by the minister of planning that "the expansive environment of the last decade has ended, and now the Saudi Arabian private sector faces normal world conditions where business success will depend on tight financial controls, high standards of product quality and service, and efficient and well planned marketing strategies." By the end of the Third Development Plan, most of the kingdom's infrastructure was in place, leading to an inevitable contraction in the construction industry. The goal now was to develop a self-sustaining private sector—moving away from trade and services toward industry and other productive activity, such as agriculture.

Figure 3
GOVERNMENT REVENUES AND EXPENDITURES
1390-1410

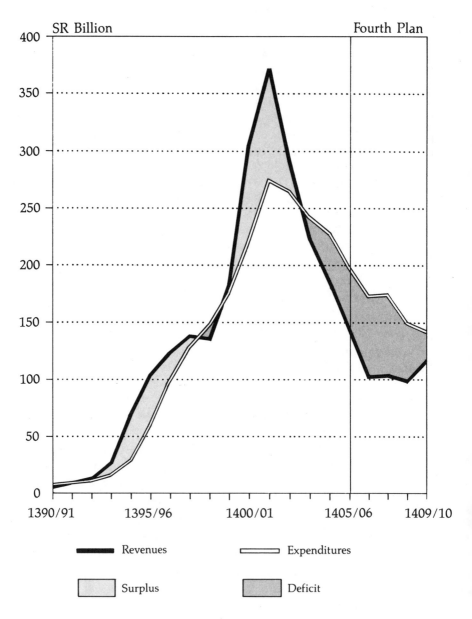

Source: Ministry of Planning, *Fifth Development Plan, 1410-1415*.

Oil revenues had declined from 85 percent of total government revenues in the first three plans to 64 percent in the Fourth Plan. The 1985-90 plan focused on improving the efficiency of existing resources, expanding nonoil revenue-generating activities (particularly in manufacturing, agriculture, and financial services), promoting private-sector initiatives to compensate for falling oil revenues—particularly activities that would increase gross domestic product rather than import and sell foreign goods—and developing a better-trained work force to reduce dependence on foreign labor. Emphasis was placed on the dispersement of activities to areas outside the main urban centers. Highest priority was given to manpower development, both to utilize Saudi resources more efficiently and to reduce reliance on foreign labor.

Two new industrial cities were to be built at Jubail on the Gulf and Yanbu on the Red Sea. Saudi Arabia's huge natural gas resources, previously burned and wasted in oil production, would provide the basic feedstock for local industry and electric power and water desalinization plants. The natural gas is now captured and processed in Jubail and transported through a pipeline to Yanbu, either for use in industry there or for export. A second, parallel pipeline carries crude oil, assuring the supply to the west coast even if sea routes were cut. Yanbu became the location of a crude oil export terminal, oil refineries for local consumption and export, a natural gas separation complex, and a petrochemicals complex. Jubail has 19 new industries, including a direct reduction steel mill, an aluminum smelter, and plants to produce methanol, fertilizer, petrochemicals, and plastics.

Agriculture, previously neglected, was to receive particular emphasis to reduce dependence on foreign foodstuffs and improve rural standards of living. Farmers received subsidies for purchases of machinery and equipment, inputs such as electricity, fertilizer, and seed below cost, and direct output subsidies, typically in the form of very high price supports. This encouragement has pushed the area under cultivation up to 7,410,000 acres and made the kingdom self-sufficient in meat, poultry, eggs, and dairy products. The incentives to wheat growers have pushed wheat production well above internal needs and locked government into a program to subsidize overpriced wheat, with the specter of depleting Saudi Arabia's precious water aquifers looming on the horizon.

The results of the third plan were mixed. By 1989 the government's dependence on petroleum resources, which until 1983 had accounted

Figure 4
GOVERNMENT EXPENDITURES 1390-1410

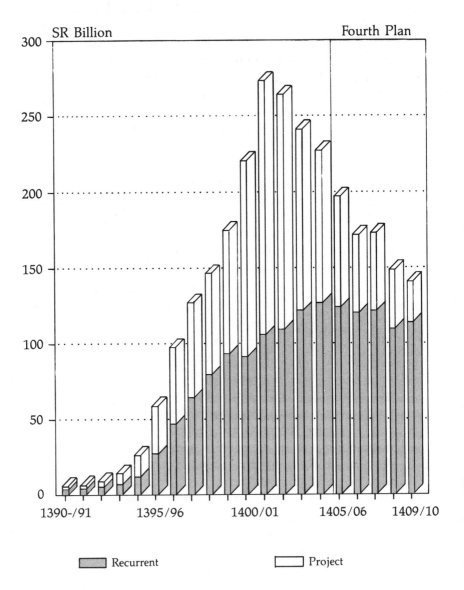

Recurrent   Project

Source: Ministry of Planning, *Fifth Development Plan, 1410-1415.*

TABLE 9
DEVELOPMENT PLAN EXPENDITURES
(in billions of Saudi Riyals)

| | 3rd plan (1400-05) | | 4th plan (1405-10) | | 5th plan (1410-15) | |
	SR	% of total	SR	% of total	SR	% of total
Economic resource development	261.8	33.4	130.7	19.0	69.9	14.0
Human resource development	129.6	16.6	135.3	19.7	141.1	28.3
Social development	61.2	7.8	89.7	13.0	87.2	17.5
Physical infrasturce	249.1	31.8	144.3	21.0	97.9	19.7
Development expenditure	701.7	89.7	500.0	72.7	396.1	79.5
Administration	31.4	4.0	70.2	10.2	102.1	20.5
Reserves & subsidies	49.6	6.3	117.3	17.1	-	-
Total civilian expenditure	782.7	100.0	687.5	100.0	498.1	100.0

Source: Ministry of Planning, *Third Development Plan, 1400-05; Fourth Development Plan, 1405-10; Fifth Development Plan, 1410-15.*

for about 50 percent of Saudi Arabia's gross domestic product (GDP) and 90 percent of government revenues, had dropped to 21 percent. Petroleum refining capacity rose substantially. The country now produces its own fuel oil, kerosene, and other products rather than send its crude oil to foreign refineries and then import refined products. Natural gas resources that were wasted earlier now fuel industrial complexes and generate electric power. In addition the government is cooperating with the United States to develop solar power.

The economy received a boost from the rise in crude oil prices following the 1988 OPEC agreement, but at a level still far below the boom years. Budget deficits continued, made up by foreign reserves. The construction industry and related service industries continued to contract, with an estimated million foreign workers leaving the country by 1987. This had an immediate impact on retailers who sold goods to the work force.

The downward spiral of oil production and prices shook the Saudis out of their psychological high. The boom years had provided an enormous boost to their self-esteem, for the world had come knocking on their door to share in their vast wealth. The new reality forced an adjustment in their outlook.

But the new situation had to be faced. The Fifth Five Year Plan (1990-95) focuses on encouraging the private sector to build on the economic foundations laid by government in the four completed plans. Priorities stress private investment that uses local raw materials and resources economically, particularly in agriculture, industry, and trade. Increasing ownership of public services is encouraged in the fields of electric power, communications, and transport. The government will promote efficiencies in production through better planning, use of appropriate technologies, and realistic assessments of costs and benefits in all on-going and future enterprises. Careful research, planning, and administration will be pursued, with stress on better training of local manpower and efficient maintenance of activities already under way.

The Intricacies of Multinational Business

This huge building of infrastructure has attracted numerous foreign businesses from America and Europe, requiring them to learn a whole new set of rules. Doing business in the kingdom is not without its hazards. Foreigners must have a local sponsor, either a government agency, or a local businessman. Saudi sponsors share profits after arranging government contracts and trading partnerships. These shares have been a major route for funneling wealth to the new elites, and through them to all levels of the middle class.

Business arrangements operate under Saudi law. Foreign businessmen should understand from the outset that their embassy and home government cannot bail them out if they run afoul of local customs and Saudi regulations.

Saudi Investment in Foreign Assets

The sudden large increase in oil prices in the 1970s caused a major shift in world monetary reserves. OPEC revenues in 1974 were so

TABLE 10
CHANGES PROMOTED BY DEVELOPMENT PLANS 1390-1410

	1970	1990	1992	To be added 1990-95
Number of students	545,000	2,842,000	1,108,000	
Number of students primary and secondary	600,000		2,690,000	
Number of colleges and institutes of high learning			82	
Number of university students		107,528		
Number of vocational and specialized students			200,000	
Number of teachers	23,000	185,000	70,000	
Number of hospitals			285	
Number of hospital beds	11,000	38,000	39,500	
Number of health care centers			2,500	
Number of physicians	1,200		20,000	
Infant mortality	148 (per 1000)	43		
Daily caloric intake	2,000	3,000+		
Number of airports			23	
Number of dams			183	
Kilometers of roads	17,000		116,511	
Number of corporations	1,000		7,000	
Number of factories	199	2,193	2,255	
Factory employees	14,000	145,000		
Electricity generation	418 megawatts	14,570 megawatts		
Daily output of desalinated water (cubic meters)	20,000		1,500,000	
Miles of roads	4,800	22,200	3,000	
Telephone lines	77,000	1,437,000	700,000	
Acres under cultivation	1,300,000	7,400,000	3,700,000	
Number of homes built		465,000		

Total spent 1970-1990: $776,000,000,000 ($65,000 per citizen)

Total to be spent 1990-95: 200,000,000,000 ($17,000 per citizen)

Source: *Christian Science Monitor*, May 15, 1990; Dr. Nasser Ibrahim Rashid and Dr. Esber Ibrahim Shaheen, Saudi Arabia and the Gulf War; Kingdom of Saudi Arabia, Fifth Development Plan 1990-1995.

large that the oil-producing countries took in $60 billion more than they could spend. Although there was considerable fear among world economists that surplus oil money from the Middle East would swamp

Figures 5
GROSS DOMESTIC PRODUCT BY MAIN SECTOR
1390-1410

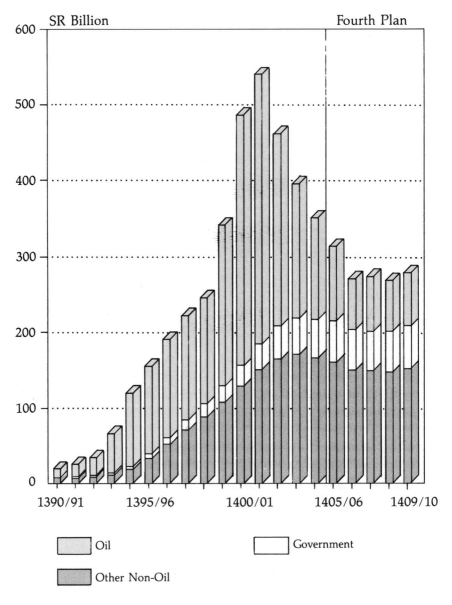

Source: Ministry of Planning, *Fifth Development Plan, 1410-1415*.

the international monetary system, the surplus cash was easily absorbed by existing banks and lending institutions in Europe, Japan, and the United States. Saudi Arabia's foreign assets grew from about $4.3 billion in 1973 to more than $145 billion in 1982. They fell from $114 billion in 1985 to an estimated $75 billion in 1989, depleted by budget deficits.

Although the Gulf War strengthened oil prices, Saudi Arabia's foreign reserves were further depleted to pay its share of the bills (approximately US$16.9 billion). The March 1991 figure for foreign assets was $54.1 billion.

Other Resources

Hydrocarbons are not Saudi Arabia's only resource. Gold has been discovered at numerous sites around the kingdom, with a mine now operating near Najran. Coal in good quantities has been found near Qasim, phosphate in the north. Evidences of silver, bauxite, copper, iron, lead, tin, and zinc are largely unexploited.

The dramatic remolding of an entire way of life in a region as harsh and hostile as Saudi Arabia is not an easy undertaking. The availability of petroleum and the unlimited capital it brings in does not change the fact that other essential resources are scarce, that huge areas are arid from lack of water, and that fresh water is a very expensive commodity to produce and transport.

Water is more vital than oil to people in such an environment. An estimated 10 percent of the kingdom's water supply is surface water, resulting from rainfall in the west and southwest. Ground water, held in aquifers, provides 84 percent, but this is a nonrenewable water source. Present projections indicate that by 1997 agriculture will be using almost all the water available in Saudi Arabia from deep aquifers. If the water resources in the kingdom's underground aquifers are to be devoted to irrigating agriculture, the growing urban demands for fresh water must be met from other sources. Desalinated sea water, which costs an estimated $2 a cubic foot, provides 5 percent of the kingdom's water supply. Daily production is about 5.5 million gallons—more than in any other country. Reclaimed waste water provides 1 percent of total needs.

The Arab nations to the north have far bleaker prospects, for they lack the financial resources to pay for expensive water. Iraq and Syria

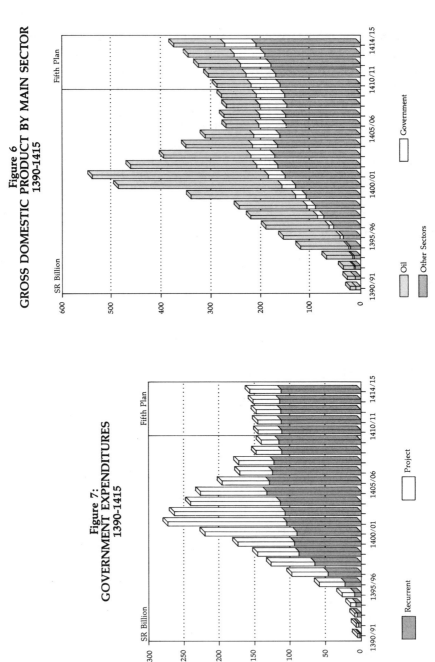

Figure 6
GROSS DOMESTIC PRODUCT BY MAIN SECTOR
1390-1415

Figure 7:
GOVERNMENT EXPENDITURES
1390-1415

Source: Ministry of Planning, *Fifth Development Plan, 1410-1415.*

Figure 8
NATIONAL WATER BALANCE
WATER RESOURCES UTILIZED

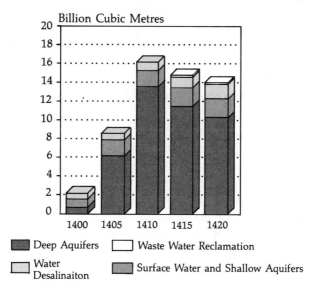

Deep Aquifers   Waste Water Reclamation

Water Desalinaiton   Surface Water and Shallow Aquifers

Figure 9
WATER DEMAND

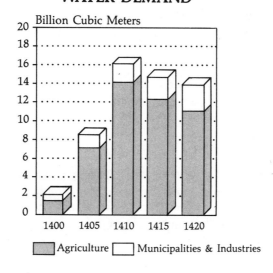

Agriculture   Municipalities & Industries

Source: Ministry of Planning, *Fifth Development Plan, 1410-1415.*

are unhappy because Turkey is diverting water from the Tigris and Euphrates Rivers with dams. Israel diverts most of the water from the Jordan, hoards the aquifers under the West Bank, and eyes the Litani River in Lebanon as a wasted resource. Egypt's population grows far faster than the fertility of the Nile valley can support. Future stability in the region may very well pivot on pressing needs for water.

The Need for Human Resource Development

No decisions are more crucial than those which determine the development of human resources, for after the oil is gone, people will remain. If Saudi leaders tried to visualize the situation in which they would like to find their people when that time comes, presumably they would aspire to a comfortable living standard that could be sustained— without oil. How can that goal be reached?

The availability of capital does not guarantee the other essentials for modernization—a skilled labor force, stable institutions, and organizational structures. Money is more easily diverted into consumption, construction, and services than channeled into new institutions and economic activities. Incorrect interpretations of Islam lead many Muslims to believe in predestination, rather than in assuming responsibility for their future. Resistance to change is strong in that part of Saudi society that is still traditional.

Nor are management skills quickly or easily grasped. Delegation of authority means surrendering power, and it takes a brave man to make difficult decisions, because a wrong decision can lead to loss of face. Exalted plans can be made and lofty intentions expressed, but action may be postponed to avoid crises.

O God! Lord of Power (and Rule), Thou givest Power to whom Thou pleasest, and Thou strippest off power from whom Thou pleasest: Thou enduest with honour whom Thou pleasest, and Thou bringest low whom Thou pleasest: In Thy hand is all Good. Verily, over all things Thou has power

Qur'an: III, 26

In the vast infrastructure that now exists in Saudi Arabia, everything from vehicle repair shops to desalinization plants must be taken over, managed, serviced, and protected from the harsh desert environment. Many of these activities involve menial or humdrum tasks that have little appeal to the upwardly mobile. The temptation is to employ foreigners for these jobs. Involving large numbers of people in completely new motivations and work patterns causes all kinds of dislocations and anxieties. Those who have focused their attention on getting rich have done very well by operating in traditional ways. But mobilizing the human resources to tackle all the nitty-gritty details of modernization has been much more difficult. People who are receiving all kinds of subsidies are not motivated to work hard, particularly at blue collar or menial tasks. Work restricts their freedom, and requires conformity. Structured employment does not mesh with some of the deeply ingrained Saudi values.

Access to "unearned incomes" (subsidies through social services) reduces the appeal of low-level, blue-collar employment, necessitating the importation of hundreds of thousands of guest workers to do menial tasks, but without any intention of assimilating them. The pro-Iraq stance some of them adopted during the Gulf War mandated a reevaluation of that policy.

Provision of Education Within Saudi Arabia

Modern education is a recent phenomenon in Saudi Arabia, and was quite deliberately undertaken by the monarchy in a conscious effort to bring the country into the modern world.

Public schooling is now available to all Saudi children (although education is not compulsory), so that the literacy rate should increase very rapidly as the current generation moves through school and older illiterates pass from the scene. Numerous technical schools and vocational training centers provide skills training. Special education programs provide training for the handicapped.

Saudi Arabia has invested huge sums in higher education, both for study abroad and in local institutions, to meet manpower requirements. The kingdom has 82 colleges and institutes of high learning. Education is segregated by sex at all ages, even at the university level where closed circuit television brings male lecturers to women students.

MAJOR UNIVERSITIES IN SAUDI ARABIA

• King Saud University in Riyadh, founded in 1957 as Riyadh University, renamed in 1982; colleges of administrative science, agriculture, agriculture and veterinary sciences (in Al Qasim), arts, computer sciences, dentistry, economics and administration (in Al Qasim), education (both in Riyadh and Abha), engineering, medicine (also in Abha and in Al Qasim), allied medical sciences, pharmacy and science; graduate studies; Center for Women's University Studies; Arabic Language Institute.

• Islamic University in Madinah, founded in 1961; faculties of Islamic Law, the Holy Quran and Islamic Studies, Dawa and Usul Al Din, Islamic Traditions, and Arabic Language.

• King Abdul Aziz University in Jiddah, founded in 1967; arts and humanities, earth sciences, economic and administration, education (in Medina), engineering, marine sciences, medicine and allied sciences, meteorology and science; Masters degrees in several of the above; Doctorates in earth sciences and education; Research and Development Center; International Center for Research in Islamic Economics; King Fahd Medical Research Center.

• Imam Muhammad ibn Saud Islamic University in Riyadh, founded in 1953, given university status in 1974; High Judiciary Institute trains sharia judges; Faculty of Shariah trains ulama; Faculty of Arabic Language and Social Science.

• King Faisal University in Dammam and Hofuf, founded in 1975; Faculties of Agriculture, Veterinary Medicine and Animal Resources at Hofuf; Faculties of Medicine and Medical Sciences, Engineering at Dammam; Community Service Center.

• King Fahd University of Petroleum and Minerals in Dhahran, founded in 1963, given university status in 1975; applied engineering, computer science and engineering, engineering science, environmental design, industrial management, sciences; College of Educational Services; Graduate School; Center of Applied Geology; Data Processing Center; Research Center.

• Umm Al Qura University in Makkah, founded in 1979; colleges of shariah and education, agricultural sciences, Arabic language, applied sciences and engineering, *Dawa and Usul al Din*, education, social sciences; Educational and Psychological Research Center; Hajj Research Center; International Center for Islamic Education, Scientific and Engineering Research Center, Scientific Research and Islamic Heritage Rejuvenation Center.

All but two (King Fahd University and Islamic University) admit women as well as men, and all have foreign as well as Saudi students. Graduates increased from 808 in 1970 to 12,501 in 1986. During the same period Saudi graduates from universities overseas increased from 0 to 2,800.

The local university system was vastly expanded so that Saudi youth would not be forced to go abroad for higher education. The quality of education in these Saudi universities has improved over the years. Graduates with high quality degrees from American or European universities still get the best positions, although degrees from King Saud University and King Fahd University rank close behind.

The economic retrenchment in the 1980s diminished the number of jobs available to new college graduates. Now the growing educated class cannot be so easily absorbed, and many new graduates are having to take jobs in the provinces. Government is emphasizing courses of study tailored to meet the nation's needs rather than the individual's preference for prestigious employment.

The Complexities of Modernization

The graduates of these many institutions are moving into a steadily growing middle class. The most visible evidence of change is the movement from nomadic tents and mud-brick dwellings to modern villas and apartments. Rising revenues have made possible an enormous amount of construction, and urban Saudis expect all the modern urban services—electricity, piped fresh water, sewage systems, radio and television, personal automobiles, multiple appliances, buses, supermarkets, and neighborhood schools. Providing the targeted standard of living for all has been a huge task. Hospitals and schools had to be built in every town, along with roads, communications networks, power, water, and sewer systems.

Providing new housing for all who wanted it presented problems when construction could not keep pace with demand. A common complaint in the 1970s was that rents were driven out of sight by foreign businesses which would pay any price to secure accommodations for their staffs. This made it very difficult for the less affluent Saudis who also wanted to move to more pleasant quarters.

Real estate development also offered the opportunity to make a fortune far more easily than in a government office or setting up a business, yet contributed far less to a stable economy. In the 1970s hotel space was at a premium, fueled by foreign businessmen, and extremely difficult to find.

Fortunately, enough construction has been completed to relieve those shortages and the competition for scarce space has slacked off as the scale of development was cut back in the 1980s. In fact, hotel construction eventually exceeded demand, causing some hotels to close.

Now that the amenities of life are easily available in Saudi Arabia, the challenge will be to keep all the mechanisms of modernization functioning. The newly educated class must gradually assume responsibility for the many tasks of management and maintenance involved in the smooth running of an industrial economy.

King Fahd turning wheel on pipeline.

Engineers and workers on an oil field installation.

Agriculture in the Kingdom.

Oil tanks on land.

Chapter 6
THE ROLE OF SAUDI ARABIA IN WORLD AFFAIRS

Saudi Arabia's foreign policy since the 1950s has reflected its rulers' concern for regional stability, their fear of radical Arab nationalism, and their devotion to Islam. Attempts to achieve Arab solidarity have often conflicted with both internal security needs and concern for the safety of petroleum exports. The Saudi leaders have sought to use their influence through quiet diplomacy to resolve inter-Arab disputes wherever possible.

The Arabian Peninsula After World War I

After World War I, Great Britain established treaties with the shaykhdoms along the coasts of the Arabian Peninsula and was the leading imperial power—guarding her sea routes to India, which circled the peninsula. A primary British fueling station was established at Aden (in what is now Yemen). Saudi Arabia's relations with Great Britain from 1925 to 1950 mainly concerned boundary disputes.[1]

Britain's unsuccessful attempt to regain control of the Suez Canal in 1956 marked a major shift in power in the Middle East. In 1968 the British government announced that its vital interests would no longer extend east of Suez, leaving a vacuum to be filled by the United States.[2]

THE QUEST FOR ARAB UNITY

The Arab League, founded in March 1945, was based on an Arab vision of a wider unity transcending national boundaries among the speakers of Arabic. The 1950s and 1960s were characterized by the efforts of Arab radicals to achieve this Arab unity, juxtaposed with a bitter rivalry between Egypt and Saudi Arabia for the leadership of the Arab world.

```
┌─────────────────────────────────────────────────────────┐
│                      TABLE 11                            │
│                 ARAB LEAGUE MEMBERS                      │
│                                                         │
│  Algeria      Jordan        Morocco       Sudan         │
│  Bahrain      Kuwait        Oman          Syria         │
│  Djibouti     Lebanon       Palestine     Saudi Arabia  │
│  Egypt        Libya         Qatar         Tunisia       │
│  Iraq         Mauritania    Somalia       Yemen         │
│                  United Arab Emirates                   │
└─────────────────────────────────────────────────────────┘
```

Initially Saudi Arabia subscribed to its neighbors' aspirations for political unity, but was wary of the geographic concept and the idea of secular government. King Saud was attracted by Egyptian President Gamal Abdul Nasser's Arab ideals, but in 1962 Nasser supported a coup against the monarchy in Yemen, while the Saudis backed the royalists. Egypt actually bombed Saudi villages along the border and kept 65,000 men mired in a guerilla war in Yemen until 1967, when another disastrous conflict with Israel resulted in Nasser's humiliation.

Radical Arab nationalists sought to use revolutionary socialism to cement together a single nation stretching from the Atlantic to the Gulf. Their hopes were boosted in 1963 when the revolutionary Baath Party seized power in both Syria and Iraq. Both new regimes sought Soviet military and economic assistance. President Nasser of Egypt, emboldened by Soviet aid programs, called for the overthrow of the traditional Arab monarchies. This stance by their radical neighbors made the kings in both Saudi Arabia and Jordan feel threatened.

Jordan was, and still is, ruled by a Hashemite dynasty descended from earlier rulers of the Hijaz. Although Abdul Aziz Ibn Saud drove the Hashemite rulers out in 1924, depriving them of their custodianship of Makkah (Mecca) and Medina, rivalries between Saudi Arabia and the Hashemite ruler of Jordan were abandoned after World War II. The Saudis provided development assistance and direct financial support to Jordan as a front-line buffer state against Israel.

The Saudis Focus on Islam as a Counter Force to Pan-Arabism

Arab unity is a modern, national concept imported from Europe in the 19th century. King Faisal of Saudi Arabia believed that nationalism, a secular concept, was divisive rather than unifying, and

> O mankind! We created you from a single (pair) of a male and a female, and made you into nations and tribes, that ye may know each other (not that ye may despise each other).
>
> Verily, the most honored of you in the sight of God is (he who is) the most righteous of you. And God has full knowledge and is well acquainted (with all things).
>
> *Qur'an: XLIX, 13*

that Muslim unity, a far older concept, was a more realistic unifying force. Islam is uniquely resistant to secularization. Its emphasis on honor and doctrinal absolutism provides a community identity that substitutes for both outdated loyalties to dying traditional groups and for emerging nationalist loyalties based on language and culture. Its theology downplays individualism and social factions. Fundamentalist Muslims expect Islamic rulers to protect the faith and enforce the law, rather than encourage pluralism and accountable government.

Although the annual pilgrimage to Makkah brought Muslims together every year, the Muslim community never had any sort of organized liaison until 1965. Then, in an effort to counter radicalism and secularism in the Arab and Muslim worlds, King Faisal of Saudi Arabia convened in Makkah a ten-day international conference of Islamic nations, which met with enthusiastic response from both the Arab states and the non-Arab Muslims of Africa and Asia.

THE MUSLIM WORLD LEAGUE

The first Islamic Conference was convened in Makkah in 1965 to bring together an Islamic body which could counter Arab radical nationalism/socialism, than rampant in Egypt and Syria.

In 1970 Islamic cooperation was put on a systematic basis. King Faisal established a Secretariat-General of the Muslim World League (also called the Organization of the Islamic Conference) in Jiddah, devoted to promoting cooperation among Muslim states, elimination of Soviet influence and radicalism in the Arab world, and the mobilization of the Muslim world behind the Arab struggle against Zionism. (Israel was regarded as an enemy as long as she occupied both Jerusalem and surrounding Arab lands.)

The periodic Islamic conferences held in different Muslim nations attracted increasing participation by many of the leading Muslim statesmen and thinkers, and specific measures were taken to solve pressing current problems. In 1975 King Faisal convened an Islamic Conference in Pakistan attended by 43 heads of Muslim states. His dream of a coherent Muslim bloc acting together in their own interests seemed realized. At that conference, for example, the Arabs and Iranians agreed on the need for dialog over all the issues in the Gulf region. Also in 1975 an Islamic Development Bank was launched with capital of over $2 billion subscribed by member states.

The Muslim World League is one of the non- governmental bodies supporting the United Nations. It is widely respected for its scholarship program, Islamic centers around the world, financial support of Muslim causes, annual international seminars in Makkah during the hajj, and various publications and periodicals in both Arabic and English.

The 1992 meeting of the Standing Committee of the Moslem World League discussed new strategies for promoting economic cooperation among Islamic countries. At a time when more and more nations are forming regional economic blocs, Saudi Arabia encouraged the Islamic states to form their own economic group to accelerate economic development and raise living standards at a faster pace.

An emergency meeting of the foreign ministers of the 47-nation group was held in Jiddah in December 1992. They urged the United Nations Security Council to use force to stop Serbian attacks on Muslims in Bosnia-Herzegovina, but rejected calls from Iran to aid the Bosnian Muslims in defiance of the UN arms embargo.

Continuing Conflicts of Interest Across the Region

The June 1967 war with Israel resulted in the capture by the Israeli army of the Golan Heights in Syria, Egypt's Sinai Peninsula, the West Bank and Gaza Strip, and East Jerusalem. This disastrous defeat ended Nasser's psychological domination of the Arab world. Egypt withdrew its troops from Yemen and left the Arabian Peninsula to Saudi authority. The Saudis then relented and normalized their relations with Egypt.

Britain withdrew from Aden in 1968, to be replaced by a radical regime in South Yemen, and from the Gulf shaykhdoms in 1970, leaving a power vacuum in the Middle East. Because the United States was preoccupied with the war in Vietnam, Iran was chosen as a surrogate to replace the United Kingdom as guardian of the region's stability, but Iran unsettled all her neighbors by forcibly seizing two islands in the Strait of Hormuz and temporarily claiming Bahrain. In that same period traditional regimes in Libya, Sudan, and Somalia were overthrown by military coups.

The Baathists in Baghdad laid claim to Kuwait and sought to undermine all the remaining conservative regimes. Marxist elements launched attempts to seize power in North Yemen and in Oman. These radical movements alarmed the Saudis.

Nasser died in 1970, and was replaced by Anwar Sadat, who shared King Faisal's interest in pan-Islamism. He expelled Soviet military advisers and stopped supporting radical groups in the Arabian Peninsula.

The Cold War Preoccupies the Superpowers

During this period, the conflict between the United States and the Soviet Union had very real effects on Saudi Arabia and her neighbors. Ever since the 1940s, when formal diplomatic relations were established, Saudi Arabia has shared with the United States a commitment to maintaining stability in a politically volatile Middle East.

SAUDI SECURITY RELATIONS WITH THE UNITED STATES

The first U.S. military mission was sent in 1943 to provide training for the Saudi army. The U. S. Corps of Engineers constructed the air field at Dhahran. The relationship expanded steadily during the cold war. In 1951 a mutual defense assistance agreement established a permanent US Military Training Mission in Saudi Arabia, which still operates.

Economic interdependence drives the relationship as well: Saudi oil is essential to Western economies; Saudi Arabia is a major customer for Western expertise, goods, and services. In return for assuring oil supplies to the United States, Saudi Arabia has been promised virtually unlimited defense cooperation. Although the inability of the United States to defend the shah of Iran, along with consistent American support of Israel, has given the Saudis occasional doubts, Iraq's invasion of Kuwait and the war that followed reassured the Saudis that the United States would stand by its commitments.

Empathy with the United States was based on oil resources, strategic location in the Middle East, and the Saudi government's stern rejection of communist doctrine. The devoutly Muslim Saudis were always dismayed by the Soviet Union's espousal of atheism, and were suspicious of Soviet intentions in the Middle East—particularly the ties between Moscow and secular regimes in the region. Saudi financial aid was given to these countries to counter Soviet influence.

Saudi dismay was intensified by the Soviet invasion of Afghanistan in 1979. Saudi Arabia provided financial support to the freedom fighters during the occupation, and continues to support a *mujahiddin* faction in Afghanistan. The Soviet withdrawal from Afghanistan in 1989 permitted the Saudis to revise their relations with the USSR. Subsequent liberalization of Soviet policy led the Saudis to receive Soviet officials in Riyadh in 1991—the first time since 1938 when the Saudi legation in Moscow was closed.

CURRENT RELATIONS WITH THE FORMER SOVIET REPUBLICS

The breakup of the Soviet Union eliminated Saudi Arabia's fear of communism. Riyadh established relations with most of the 15 separate Soviet republics in 1990, and growing numbers of Muslims from the former Soviet Union were permitted to make the annual pilgrimage to Makkah. The Saudis donated one million copies of the Quran to Soviet Muslims, with Aeroflot and Saudia, their national airlines, splitting the transportation burden.

Negotiations were undertaken in 1992 to sell surplus Saudi wheat in the new Union, preferably in some sort of barter deal. Saudi Arabia has generally sold its surplus wheat to oil-exporting countries outside of OPEC (Norway, China, the UK, Egypt), a strategy to encourage trading relations with countries that affect the oil market.

The Conflict with Israeli Dominates Arab Politics

The conflict with Israel was a unifying force in the Arab world after 1970. The Saudis have always supported the cause of the 6 million Palestinians, both the 2.4 million who live in Israel and the occupied territories and the 3.6 million who live elsewhere. The conflict is not with Judaism, for the Jews, like the Christians, are regarded by Muslims as "people of the Book" (who believe in revealed scripture which Muslims also venerate). The conflict is with Zionism—the belief that the Jews have a right to their ancient homeland because of an equally ancient religious covenant. The failure to resolve the grievances of the Palestinians has resulted in a half century of conflict and instability in the Middle East.

> Those who believe (in the Quran), and those who follow the Jewish (scriptures), and the Christians and the Sabians,—and who believe in God and the Last Day, and work righteousness, shall have their reward with their Lord: on them shall be no fear, nor shall they grieve.
>
> *Qur'an: II, 62*

Saudi kings believe that American support of Zionism was a major factor in radicalizing the Arab world. The creation of the new state of Israel as a home for Jews persecuted in Europe in the 1930s won sympathy in the West, but was viewed in the Arab world as the forcible dispossession by an immigrant power of the Palestinians, who had peopled the land for centuries. Arabs saw only twisted logic in making the Palestinians pay for the crimes of the Nazis—depriving Arabs of the right to self-determination and subjecting them to a government not of their choosing.

The United States was too hamstrung by its rivalry with the Soviet Union to pay close attention to passions in the Third World. Israel was regarded as a democratic ally, strongly anti-communist in sentiment, in a dangerously volatile region. But United States support of Israel gave Arabs the impression that they didn't matter in the West.

Arab defeat by the Israelis three times in 20 years (1948, 1956, 1967) forced the Arabs to recognize their own weakness and stagnation. Pride made them search for culprits. Was the Arab social order defective? Was the fault with the Arab regimes fighting Israel? Were they weak and needed strengthening? Had Arab society degenerated by turning away from Islam? Was there Western racial bias against the Arabs?

The last explanation gave the most comfort to Arab pride. Periodic controversies between the American President and Congress during the 1970s and 1980s over arms sales to Saudi Arabia fueled Saudi perceptions of overwhelming Israeli influence in Washington. The Saudis interpreted the denial of arms as a weakening of the American commitment to defend Saudi Arabia, and decried Washington's failure to maintain an evenhanded stance.

TABLE 12
COMPARATIVE POPULATIONS

Jewish population worldwide	17,000,000
Population of Israel	4,636,000
Jewish population in United States	5,935,000
(2.4% of total US population)	
Palestinian population worldwide	6,000,000
Palestinians in Israel and Occupied Territories	2,400,000
Muslim population worldwide	1,000,000,000
Population of Arab countries	215,000,000
Muslim population in United States	6,000,000

Source: *The World Almanac and Book of Facts* 1992.

TABLE 13
ESTIMATED AMERICAN SUPPORT OF ISRAEL

Annual donations (tax deductible) from private US citizens to Israel	$1,000,000,000
Annual sale of Israeli bonds in US	500,000,000
Annual commercial loans from US banks to Israel	1,000,000,000
US Government annual military and economic aid	4,000,000,000
Total annual private and public assistance	6,500,000,000
Annual assistance on per capita basis	$ 1,300
Total annual Israeli gross national product	24,000,000,000
Percentage of GNP coming from US assistance	25%

Source: *The Washington Report on Middle East Affairs*, November 1992.

When another war broke out in 1973 between the Israelis and the Arabs, Saudi Arabia and Egypt cooperated in imposing an oil embargo on Israel's supporters, with far-reaching economic impact in the West (discussed in Chapter 5). Substantial financial support was provided to the Palestinians. The Saudis did not, however, support the separate

Egyptian peace with Israel in 1978. They opposed the Camp David accords after President Carter refused to let an Islamic commission study them to test their practicalities. Saudi Arabia joined the other Arab states in condemning Egypt and breaking diplomatic relations.

Major Power Shifts in the 1970s and 1980s

During the 1970s the principal external threat to Saudi Arabia's security came from her Gulf neighbors, Iraq and Iran. Great Britain had terminated her long- time presence in the Gulf. Iraq and Iran were building up their military forces—Iraq with Soviet weapons and training missions, Iran with American weapons and advisers. The Shah of Iran, who was supposedly looking after Western interests in the Gulf, was deposed in a revolution in 1979 as the Camp David accords were being finalized, terminating American influence in Tehran. Arab leaders were horrified when the United States was unable to save her surrogate or to free the American hostages seized by students in Tehran. A series of hijackings, kidnappings, and car bombings followed as the new government in Iran sought to spread its religious revolution to other Muslim nations.

The Iranian revolution transformed the balance of power in the Gulf. Its ripple effect spread far beyond the Middle East, for, like the Afghans, the Iranians successfully defied bipolar superpower politics. A people who had been overwhelmed by Western technology and materialism turned back to religion as a weapon with which to strike back at the United States and regain their self-esteem. This model of defiance has had great appeal ever since in some parts of the Muslim world.

Saudi Arabia, in contrast, had been able to provide for the economic needs of its people within the framework of its own cultural heritage, avoiding secular government and popular disenchantment with unfulfilled expectations. This stability and the interests shared with the United States made it appropriate that the kingdom should become America's major strategic ally in the Middle East. Because the United States saw the Soviet Union as the principal threat to regional security and oil supplies, the Saudis were able to buy sophisticated American military equipment, often over Israeli objections.

After making peace with Israel, President Sadat of Egypt was assassinated by militant opponents. Then in 1981 Israel bombed

Baghdad's nuclear plant, without provoking any protest from the United States. The Saudi leaders pondered the direction of American policy.

King Fahd initiated efforts to achieve a comprehensive peace settlement between the Arabs and the Israelis in 1981 by announcing a wide-ranging peace initiative that would for the first time recognize Israel's right to exist. He called for Israeli withdrawal from the West Bank and Gaza Strip, the dismantling of Jewish settlements in the occupied territories, the establishment of an independent Palestinian state with East Jerusalem as its capital, and just compensation for Palestinians dispossessed of their lands. Other Arab leaders required more time to accept the Saudi concept, but consensus in the Arab League was announced at a summit meeting a year later.[3]

During the 1980s, Saudi Arabia provided substantial financial backing to a number of other Arab governments, both in the Middle East and the Horn of Africa. The PLO and the countries that border Israel were generously financed, both as a moral obligation to the Palestinians and with the hope of encouraging the more moderate Palestinian leaders to prevail over the radical elements.

This was a period of frightening instability in the Middle East. With the Shah of Iran gone, the United States sought a new balance of power. The Soviet invasion of Afghanistan in 1979 led President Carter to publicly reaffirm vital American interests in the Gulf. That same year an agreement was reached with the Sultan of Oman giving the United States military access to an island in the Arabian Sea and airfields within Oman. In 1983 the United States created a rapid deployment force and sold sophisticated surveillance planes to Saudi Arabia.

War Between Iraq and Iran

The confusion of the Iranian revolution coupled with the inflammatory rhetoric coming out of Tehran led Iraq to lay claim in 1980 to the Shatt al Arab waterway (which formed part of their mutual border). The quarrel between the two countries culminated in an inconclusive eight-year war. The Saudis faced a dilemma in deciding whether to take sides in the conflict.

Over the years Saudi relations with Iraq have blown hot and cold. Ties were strained in 1960s and early 1970s by the radicalism of Iraq's Baathist leadership. In the mid-1970s Baghdad began moderating its policies, permitting tensions to ease. Relations were relatively stable at time of the 1979 revolution in Iran. Both the Iraqis and the Saudis, with Shiite populations of their own, felt threatened by the extremism of the Iranian revolutionaries who had seized control in Tehran.

The Saudis announced neutrality in the Iraq-Iran quarrel in 1980, and took measures to draw closer to their neighbors. Saudi relations with the small oil-producing states along the Persian Gulf have always been close. War on her northern borders led the Saudis to take the lead in the creation of the Gulf Cooperation Council (GCC) in 1981. Its six members—Saudi Arabia, Kuwait, Bahrain, the United Arab Emirates, Qatar, and Oman—came together initially to promote economic and industrial cooperation, but security concerns soon predominated.

THE GULF COOPERATION COUNCIL

GCC members participated in joint military exercises and shared intelligence data. Approximately $2 billion was invested in upgrading military forces in Oman and Bahrain. Suspicions of Iranian terrorism were heightened by a series of assassinations, car/truck bombings, and airplane hijackings. In 1984 a small rapid deployment force of 10,000 to 13,000 soldiers was created, based in Saudi Arabia (with the Saudis contributing the largest share of funds and men).

Such forces needed modern weapons. Congressional opposition to the sale of advanced American weapons in 1987 led the Saudis to turn to Britain as a major source of arms. The refusal of United States, because of Israeli opposition, to supply modern missiles, led Saudi Arabia to purchase longer-range missiles from China, leading to diplomatic differences with the United States in 1988.

The six members of the Gulf Cooperation Council also laid the foundation for a potential "Gulf Arab common market" in which goods and workers would move freely across borders. As economic issues increased in importance, the heads of government met regularly to develop policy. Tariffs and job restrictions were to be phased out, aid and jointly financed industrial projects undertaken.

In spite of its neutrality, Saudi Arabia provided $27 billion in low-interest loans and grants to Iraq during the war with Iran, permitted use of the Red Sea port of Al Qadimah to bring in East European and Soviet military equipment, provided oil from the Neutral Zone, and assisted in constructing a pipeline to transport 2 million bpd of Iraqi oil across its territory.

In 1986 Iran began blocking shipping in the Gulf to prevent supplies from reaching Iraq and Iraqi oil from being exported. Kuwait approached both the United States and the Soviet Union to protect its tankers. American policy in this period was to prevent any one country from gaining control of the oil resources in the Gulf, while maintaining its commitment to protect Israel. By the close of 1987 the American and six other navies had responded to this threat to tanker shipments through the Gulf by convoying and other measures to thwart Iranian minelaying operations and missile attacks. Saudi minesweepers and AWACs aircraft aided this effort, but the Saudis supported United Nations efforts to negotiate a ceasefire. All GCC members were relieved when Iran agreed in 1988 to UN Resolution 598 and an end to the conflict.

A Shift in the Superpower Equation

The Soviet withdrawal from Afghanistan in 1989 represented a major shift in the world balance of power, and with it came a marked decrease in Soviet support for Third World leaders eager to confront the United States. Although the breakup of the Soviet Union would take many more months, President Gorbachev recognized that his country had stretched its imperial aspirations far beyond its faltering economic capacity. Unlimited military and economic aid was no longer available to client states all over the world. Nor would the Soviet Union any longer thwart coordinated international action by the United Nations against aggression.

THE GULF WAR USHERS IN A NEW ERA
OF INTERNATIONAL COOPERATION

In spite of this changed situation, Iraq's dictator, Saddam Hussein, gave the region very little respite. He soon made it clear that he expected Kuwait and Saudi Arabia to forgive the $42 billion they had provided to his war effort, and to provide him with billions more to compensate for his loss of income from oil sales during his war with Iran. He also claimed that Kuwait was exporting more than her OPEC quota (thus depressing oil prices and depriving Iraq of income), as well as impinging on Iraqi territory and stealing oil from the Rumaila oilfield which straddles the border.

Repeated meetings and efforts to mediate the dispute by King Fahd and other leaders were of no avail. The Iraqi army invaded and occupied Kuwait in August 1990. Saddam Hussein announced that Kuwait had historically been part of Iraq and declared it to be Iraq's 19th province.

The Iraqi Threat to Saudi Arabia

Iraq's invasion of Kuwait was a nightmare for the Saudis. Iraq had a well-armed, seasoned army of a million men, backed up by 5,500 tanks and 500 fighter planes. Saudi Arabia had 65,000 troops, 500 tanks, and 500 planes. Much larger forces would be needed to defend the kingdom if Saddam Hussein should decide to push south out of Kuwait into Saudi Arabia's oil fields. The Saudis immediately went to the United Nations Security Council.

Because of the importance of petroleum to Western economies, the United States has regarded Saudi Arabia as part of its vital interests ever since World War II. President Bush immediately demanded that the Iraqis withdraw, as did President Gorbachev of the former Soviet Union. This extraordinary new unanimity between the superpowers permitted the UN Security Council to condemn the invasion and impose economic sanctions on Iraq. Five days after the attack King Fahd announced that he would accept United States assistance to prevent the Iraqis from moving further. President Bush took the lead in lining up a multi-national United Nations force to assist Saudi Arabia and to expel the Iraqis from Kuwait.

The success of Desert Shield and Desert Storm depended very much on the cooperation and support of the Saudis. Fortunately, major military facilities had been built in Saudi Arabia during the 1980s and equipped with an eye toward use by friendly forces in any future emergency. King Khalid Military City, constructed to house 50,000 people at a cost of $5.2 billion, was completed in 1985, located in the desert 350 miles northeast of Riyadh. Airfields with redundant runways were available. Hardware was stockpiled, all of which was essential to the successful prosecution of Desert Shield. The Saudis also provided deep-water ports to receive American troops, warehouses to store supplies, thousands of trucks and buses to move troops to their bases, transport trucks to move tanks to front lines, tents to house troops, mess halls and mobile fast-food canteens to supply fresh food.

TABLE 14
PEAK PERSONNEL STRENGTHS OF COUNTRIES
PARTICIPATING IN DESERT STORM
(including air, ground, and naval forces)

1.	Afghanistan	300	22. Norway	50
2.	Argentina	300	23. Oman	6,300
3.	Australia	700	24. Pakistan	4,900
4.	Bahrain	400	25. Philippines	Unknown
5.	Bangladesh	2,200	26. Poland	200
6.	Belgium	400	27. Qatar	2,600
7.	Canada	2,000	28. Romania	Unknown
8.	Czechoslovakia	200	29. Saudi Arabia	100,000
9.	Denmark	100	30. Senegal	500
10.	Egypt	36,000	31. Sierra Leone	200
11.	France	14,600	32. Singapore	Unknown
12.	Germany	Unknown	33. South Korea	200
13.	Greece	200	34. Spain	500
14.	Hungary	50	35. Sweden	Unknown
15.	Italy	1,200	36. Syria	19,000
16.	Japan	Unknown	37. Thailand	Unknown
17.	Kuwait	9,900	38. Turkey	Unknown
18.	Morocco	1,300	39. United Arab Emirates	4,300
19.	Netherlands	600	40. United Kingdom	45,400
20.	New Zealand	Unknown	41. United States	541,400
21.	Niger	480	42. Zaire	Unknown

Total 796,480 troops, supported by 4,000 tanks, 1,800 aircraft, and 100 warships

Source: *U. S. Department of Defense*

Desert Storm Defeats Iraq

After six months of buildup of the Allied Forces, a United Nations deadline for withdrawal from Kuwait was set, but ignored by Iraq. An air offensive was begun in January 1991. The first Iraqi planes were shot down by Captain Ayedh Al Shamrani of the Saudi Air Force. When Iraq failed to meet the final UN deadline for withdrawal, the ground offensive began on February 23. Saudi troops and those of other Arab nations, commanded by Prince Khalid bin Sultan bin Abdul Aziz, participated in both bombing runs and the ground offensive, and led

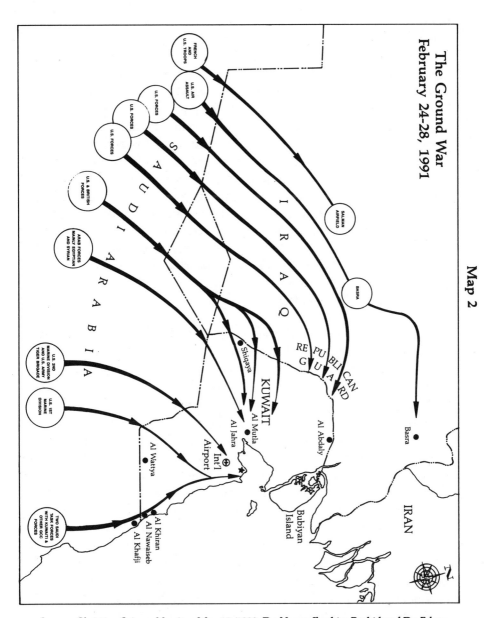

Source: *Christian Science Monitor*, May 15, 1990; Dr. Nasser Ibrahim Rashid and Dr. Esber Ibrahim Shaheen, Saudi Arabia and the Gulf War; Kingdom of Saudi Arabia, Fifth Development Plan 1990-1995.

the forces which liberated Kuwait. Within 100 hours the Iraqi army was in full retreat and a cease-fire had been accepted.

Although the Saudis attributed the outpouring of assistance from many nations and the success of the offensive against Iraq to the providence of God, Desert Storm shook the proud Arabians in many ways. The reception of foreign forces into the kingdom was a trauma in itself. The ulama tolerated this intrusion when promised that foreign military personnel would be kept away from Saudi civilians and required to obey Saudi law. Saudi women were as shocked as their men to learn that 10 percent of the American forces were women, who had left their homes and families to fight a war on foreign soil. New rules had to be formulated about how they should dress and where they could go, about what the foreign troops could receive in the way of reading material from home, about military chaplains wearing crosses and conducting services of other faiths in the heartland of Islam.

Impact of the Gulf War

After Desert Storm, the members of Gulf Cooperation Council met with Egypt and Syria. The Damascus Declaration, issued on March 6, 1991, provided an outline for increased political and economic cooperation among the eight countries. The Gulf states turned back to Western powers, however, for their immediate security needs.

Agreements were quickly worked out between the United States, Britain, and France on the one hand and Kuwait, Oman, Bahrain, and the United Arab Emirates on the other, providing access to ports, airfields, and stockpiled equipment as a deterrent to future aggression in the Gulf. Similar understandings concerning security arrangements were reiterated between the United States and Saudi Arabia (as they have been for several decades). Joint military exercises have been conducted to remind neighboring countries of these security arrangements.

The eight countries which had met in Damascus reiterated a year later their commitment to the Damascus Declaration as "a guideline to a new Arab system" to be implemented under the auspices of the Arab League, and invited other Arab states to join the group. Full support was given to negotiations to end the Arab-Israeli conflict and find a final solution for the Palestinian question.

In March and again at their September 1992 meeting the foreign ministers condemned Iraq for refusing to comply with the UN Security Council resolutions ending the Gulf War or to accept UN efforts to demarcate the border between Iraq and Kuwait. To protect the Kurds of Iraq, the foreign ministers approved a no-fly zone south of the 32nd parallel in Iraq. They expressed concern over Iran's aggressive policy towards the islands in the Strait of Hormuz, and they reiterated the claim of the United Arab Emirates over those islands. Support was expressed for United Nations efforts to end conflicts in Somalia and Yugoslavia (Bosnia-Herzegovina), and for the resumption of Middle East peace talks.

These declarations reflected major changes, brought about by Desert Storm, in the way Arab leaders view each other, depending on their stand in the Gulf War. These viewpoints reflect the cleavages among the Arab leadership between those who are blatantly anti-western (Iran, Iraq, Libya, for example), those who equivocated (Jordan, Yemen, the PLO), and those who welcomed western assistance in driving Iraq from Kuwait. The feelings of mistrust and betrayal incurred during the Gulf War have caused the Saudis to adopt a strong isolationist stance.

New Relationships Among the Arabs

Saudi sentiment toward Saddam Hussein is obvious. Immediately after the end of the hostilities, King Fahd invited Iraqi opposition groups seeking to overthrow the Iraqi dictator to a well-publicized meeting in Riyadh. Presumably these groups are receiving Saudi financial assistance as well.

Egypt and Saudi Arabia have drawn closer as a result of the Gulf War. Diplomatic relations between the two had been restored in 1987, after the Arab League agreed that members could do so at their discretion. Egyptian troops sent to assist Saudi Arabia against Iraq were much appreciated, and subsequent Saudi financial support is crucial to Egypt's faltering economy.

Acceptance of this assistance has led to controversy in Egypt because liberals fear Saudi encouragement of conservative Islamic groups in Egypt. The Saudis finance the pilgrimage to Makkah for fundamentalist students, spread conservative religious ideas among the million Egyptians who work in Saudi Arabia, influence the Egyptian media, and support Egyptians who want a return to Islamic law. Liberal

Egyptians suspect Saudi encouragement for resegregating the sexes in the recent move to provide separate buses for women in Cairo.

Syria surprised the world by backing Saudi Arabia in Desert Storm. Syria is governed by Baath socialists, but their enmity for Saddam Hussein and his Iraqi Baathists exceeded their differences with Saudi Arabia. Syria had lost Soviet financial and military assistance, and Syria's President Hafez al Asad moved shrewdly to secure possible future financial aid from both the Saudis and the United States.

Jordan's refusal to confront Iraq in the Gulf War shocked the Saudis. Jordan had become so dependent on trade with Iraq that the conflict placed the country in a hopeless economic situation. King Hussain of Jordan also had to deal with a population that was over half Palestinian. Saddam Hussein very cleverly used fiery Arab rhetoric to convince the Palestinians that he was standing up against greedy Western nations—waging war on their behalf against the sponsors of Israel. The Palestinian leadership spoke out against the United Nations coalition, putting the Jordanian monarch in a difficult doublebind.

As a result, Palestinian and Jordanian guest workers were encouraged to leave the kingdom and all grants to Jordan terminated (which amounted to 15 percent of Jordan's budget). Low-priced oil sales were discontinued, and imports from Jordan restricted. King Hussain, in the hope of mending relations with Saudi Arabia, eventually denounced Saddam Hussein, but relations between the two kingdoms are still strained.

The secular nationalists who run the Palestinian Liberation Organization are now seen as tired and tainted. Attention has recently been captured by a newer radical Palestinian organization named Hamas—the Islamic Resistance Movement, formed in 1987 to support the *intifada* in the territories occupied by Israel. It opposes any Palestinian concessions to Israel and has carried out a number of successful attacks against Israelis. Twelve hundred of its supporters were rounded up in December 1992, and over 400 alleged Islamic militants deported across the Lebanese border, disrupting peace negotiations. Moderate Palestinians argue that Israel's best counter to the Islamists' popularity would be to permit active PLO involvement in the peace process in order to make some tangible progress.

Hamas' strong Islamic orientation has won the support of many Arabs who are frustrated by the intractability of the conflict with Israel. Its leaders are present in the occupied territories, unlike the exiled PLO leadership, and it runs an efficient network of honest welfare and relief institutions for the Palestinians. In spite of links with Iran, the Saudis also provide substantial financial support to Hamas as a way to remind critics at home of their unswerving loyalties to the principles of Islam. After the expulsion of the alleged Hamas leaders from Israel and the UN Security Council demand that they be returned, the Saudi Council of Ministers issued a statement demanding the implementation of all UN resolutions—not just those pertaining to Iraq.

Relations with Yemen were also soured by the Gulf War. Saudi Arabia was always mistrustful of the Marxist government in South Yemen. The Saudis favored the overthrow of that regime until 1976, when diplomatic relations were finally established. The Saudis also monitored carefully the unification of the two Yemens into the Yemen Republic in 1990 because it would enlarge the area controlled by the ruling Yemeni Socialist Party. Various Yemeni political groups have received clandestine Saudi funds. Yemen's neutral stance in the Gulf War and its refusal to support the United Nations sanctions or use of force led Saudi Arabia to terminate economic assistance and the guest worker privileges of nearly 1,000,000 Yemeni workers from the kingdom. Most of them returned home.

Saudi Arabia and Iran Jockey for Position

Revolutionary Iran is still the biggest question mark in the region's balance of power. The Gulf War demonstrated that Arab unity does not guarantee cooperation in the Middle East. Saudi Arabia's security requires the containment of Iraq. Because Iran has the same objective, after Desert Storm the Saudis and Iranians cautiously and nervously began moving in the direction of normalizing relations with each other.

Relations with Iran have always been tinged by the ancient religious schism between the Sunnis and the Shiites. Iran is predominantly Shiite, with ultimate authority vested in the religious hierarchy that the Shias place between God and man. Saudi Arabia is predominantly Sunni, its clergy interpreting law rather than formulating it. The Saudis believe that fanatic Iranian Shiites incite and exploit discontent among Saudi Shiites who live in the oil-rich Eastern Province. The 1979 Islamic revolution in Iran brought to power militant Shiite theocrats whom the Saudi Salafi consider heretical. Moreover, Iranian officials have from time to time denounced all other governments in the area as unIslamic.

The Iranians regarded the hajj as a legitimate opportunity to proselytize. A serious clash between Iranian pilgrims and Saudi security forces during the annual pilgrimage to Makkah in 1987 reignited old enmities. More than 150,000 Iranians were present, resulting in an Iranian demonstration which sparked violent riots. The death toll reached 402, among them 275 Iranians. In the following days mass demonstrations occurred in Tehran, the Saudi embassy there was sacked, and Iranian leaders vowed to overthrow the Saudi government.

The Saudi response was to sever diplomatic relations with Tehran, at the same time increasing the influence of the religious authorities within Saudi Arabia. Security forces were bolstered and new defensive equipment purchased—AWACS, Tornado fighter-bombers, Hawk trainer aircraft from UK; CSS-2 medium-range missiles from China. The Saudi military command structure was modernized and the manufacture of avionics and telecommunications equipment undertaken. Government-funded development in the Eastern Province was accelerated, giving more social and religious equality to the Shiite population in order to dampen the appeal of pro-Iranian factions within the kingdom.

Ayatollah Khomeini, who led the religious revolution in Iran, died in 1989, and President Hashemi Rafsanjani thereafter indicated his desire to improve relations and end Iran's isolation. Then the unexpected threat posed when Iraq invaded Kuwait in 1990 led Riyadh to reevaluate its regional security concerns in 1991 and to seek a rapprochement with Iran to counterbalance the Iraqi threat. Tehran backed Saudi demands for Iraqi withdrawal from Kuwait. A compromise was reached that permitted Iranians to participate in the 1991 and 1992 hajjs, followed by a restoration of diplomatic relations. In June 1991 the Saudi foreign minister went to Tehran, the first visit by a Saudi official in 12 years.

Since then Iran has been seeking to expand its oil exports in an effort to fund its enormous development needs and to rebuild its military defense system after the punishing 95-month war it fought against Saddam Hussein. Tanks, missiles, and modern aircraft have been purchased from communist and former communist countries. The purchase of two diesel-powered submarines in 1992 (contracted by the USSR before its breakup) led to a United States protest, which failed to halt the sale. Media commentary portrays the Iranian buildup as alarming, but the Gulf states are spending far more than Iran on military equipment. Iran's substantial population and the stridency of Iranian rhetoric seem threatening to the leaders of the Gulf states. Israel, whose leaders feel it in their interest to try to destabilize the Gulf, magnifies the threat.

Correct information is difficult to sift out of the continuous media speculation, much of it written by journalists who either conceal ideological motives or whose lack of experience in Middle Eastern affairs makes them poor interpreters of daily events. Clearly a political struggle is going on within Iran between President Rafsanjani and his pragmatic supporters and the revolutionary extremists. Until he wins this political struggle, all the GCC countries have reason to remain wary of Iran's long-standing ambition to dominate the Gulf.

Exaggerated reports concerning Iran's military buildup, Iran's clumsy and aggressive policy towards the island of Abu Musa, and its support for militant religious factions across the region have all slowed significantly the important drive for rapprochement between the kingdom and Iran. The radical rhetoric emanating from Tehran (and at times from Rafsanjani himself) has done little to ameliorate the situation.

The tenor of the relationship between Saudi Arabia and Iran will determine how the future unrolls in the Gulf. If the two states can communicate and agree to cooperate, then some degree of stability should be achieved. If, on the other hand, conflicting political ideologies prevail over pragmatism and good sense, then instability and turbulence seem sure to prevail.

EFFORTS TO PROMOTE REGIONAL PEACE AND STABILITY

Within the Arab world Saudi Arabia is considered moderate. The Saudi leaders move cautiously. They have frequently acted as peacemaker. In 1987 they brought together the rulers of Morocco and Algeria to discuss their quarrel over the Saharan people's independence movement (Polisario). They sought to end the conflict in Lebanon and effect the withdrawal of all foreign forces. When the Lebanese National Assembly was unable to meet in Beirut because of military clashes and political violence, King Fahd moved the entire body to Taif in Saudi Arabia, where a reform plan was negotiated. The Saudis have encouraged talks between the PLO and Syria. Crown Prince Abd Allah's connection with the Shammar tribe, which straddles the border, has made him a very useful emissary to Syria.

On regional issues, Saudi Arabia has supported the standard Arab position, working behind the scenes to reach consensus. Saudi leaders have encouraged the series of multinational peace talks between the Arab states and Israel which began in Madrid in 1992. Generous economic assistance has been provided to Muslim states in Africa and Asia and to the PLO, with the assumption that the recipients would support Saudi policy and goals. The Saudis were shocked when Jordan, the PLO, and the two Yemens sided with Iraq in the Gulf War. Their hopes that Islam could be the vehicle for promoting Arab unity went awry because most Muslim countries have secular governments and do not base their foreign policies on religious principles.

To the Saudi kings the distinction between developed and developing countries was never as important as that between God-fearing and Godless nations. Solidarity with Muslim countries has always been an important aspect of Saudi foreign policy. Aid was directed to Muslim states—25 nations in Asia, 38 in Africa—by virtue of their creed rather than their economic circumstances. Assistance went both to neighbors and to Muslim countries further afield—Bangladesh, Pakistan, Somalia—because of religious affinity.

The chasm between the wealthy oil states and the rest of the Middle East is very striking. The poorest countries have the highest rates of population growth, which exacerbates the problems of poverty. Saudi Arabia has sought to encourage the economic and social development of these struggling Muslim countries, providing 66 billion dollars in aid to other Arab states between 1970 and 1991. Through its Saudi Fund for Development, established in 1974, the kingdom has financed projects in 63 countries, with particular emphasis on transportation assistance, agricultural development, social infrastructure, and energy. Aid to non-Islamic nations was a reward generally for their opposition to the expansion of radical socialism, which the Saudis viewed as a common threat. External grants and aid in the period between 1973 and 1981 reached 7.7 percent of the kingdom's gross national product (GNP). That level could not be maintained, but aid programs consumed 4.0 percent of GNP in 1990—far higher than the UN's suggested standard of 0.7 percent. In comparison, United States development assistance has fallen to 0.24 percent of GNP, while Japanese development assistance is 0.34 percent. Total Saudi aid disbursements are exceeded only by the United States, but the percentage of Saudi GNP channeled into aid donations is the highest of all the nations in the world.

TABLE 15
SAUDI ARABIA'S CONTRIBUTION TO
REGIONAL AND INTERNATIONAL ORGANIZATIONS

	Percent of total funds
Islamic Bank for Development	25.3
Arab Fund for Economic and Social Development	22.9
Arab Monetary Fund	14.5
OPEC Fund for International Development	30.1
Arab Bank for Economic Development in Africa	24.2
African Development Bank	0.25
World Bank	3.32
International Development Agency	3.5
International Finance Corporation	1.37
Mutual Investment Guarantee Agency	3.14
International Monetary Fund	3.6
African Development Fund	3.4
International Fund for Agricultural Development	14.25
Arab Corporation for Investment Guarantee	15
Arab Gulf Program for support of United Nations humanitarian and development organizations	76
Arab Fund for Technical Aid to Arab and African Countries	22.6
Program for Curing River Blindness	8.36
Program for combatting drought in the Sahel Countries	54

Source: *Ministry of Finance and National Economy*

Some of these programs are carried on under the auspices of the United Nations. Prince (later King) Faisal represented Saudi Arabia at its founding, and was active at United Nations meetings for many years thereafter. Saudi Arabia has always been proud of its role in and its contributions to United Nations programs.

Saudi Arabia as a Leader in the Muslim World

The world today is in a state of transition, grappling with the end of the Cold War, the breakup of the Soviet Union, and new environmental imperatives. Add to these external factors the resurgence of Islam across North Africa, the Middle East, and Central Asia. More than 45 million Muslims live in the former republics of the USSR—17 percent of the total population. China has 14 million Muslims. The appeal of the faith unsettles regions far beyond the Arab world.

Saudi Arabia is caught up in the incoherence of a rapidly changing world. Saddam Hussein still wields his fierce, inflexible power on her northern border. Iran preaches radical populist Islam and flexes its muscles just across the Gulf. The Saudis are dismayed by ethnic conflicts in the republics of Central Asia. They are horrified by the repression of the Muslim population of Bosnia-Herzegovina.

Pressures for more representative government have reached the fringes of the Arabian Peninsula. An election was held in Kuwait in October 1992, in which voting was carefully confined to about 75,000 Kuwaitis who could prove their residence since the 1920s. Nevertheless, opponents of the ruling Al Sabah family won 35 of the 50 seats in the new parliament. Bahrain, Qatar, and Oman are experiencing strong pressures for increased political participation.

The Saudis who would like more say in running their own kingdom watch these developments avidly. Their rulers must grapple with the hard realities involved in maintaining political stability and achieving regional security. In this context King Fahd has announced plans to establish a consultative parliament, has appointed its speaker, and is selecting its members.

FOOTNOTES

[1]Before the discovery of oil, borders between the various Gulf shaykhdoms were insignificant save where water and grazing rights were important. After the discovery of oil, borders became suddenly of major importance and border disputes arose between Saudi Arabia and Iraq, Abu Dhabi, and Oman. Many of these border issues have been gradually settled through negotiation.

[2]Since that time, British relations with Saudi Arabia have been confined to supplying skilled workers and military hardware, with British companies participating in Saudi development plans.

[3]The proposal was immediately rejected by Israel. Several more years passed before the PLO, in 1989, accepted Israel's right to exist and disavowed terrorism, setting the first stage for peace negotiations.

King Abdul Aziz meeting with President Roosevelt in 1945.

King Fahd visits Allied forces.

King Fahd with President Mubarak.

The Custodian of the Two Holy Mosques, King Fahd Bin Abdul Aziz with President George Bush and Saudi Ambassador to the U.S. Prince Bandar Bin Sultan Bin Abdul Aziz.

King Fahd awards a trophy during the fifth World Youth Soccer Cup Championship held in Riyadh.

Camel racing attracts thousands of spectators during the National Heritage and Cultural Festival.

Chapter 7
SAUDI ARABIA APPROACHES THE 21ST CENTURY

People everywhere in the world strive for accomplishments in which they can take pride. In many parts of the world these efforts are directed, not toward upward mobility and the acquisition of material possessions, but rather toward intangible rewards such as titles, intellectual discoveries, or a reputation for wisdom or bravery. In Saudi Arabia the Bedouin valued those traits which were appropriate to their stark desert environment—honor, courage, hospitality, and loyalty to kin. These ancient nomadic virtues were supplemented over the centuries by the ethical values of Islam, which mandated brotherhood and a deep veneration of religious law to guide social conduct.

Every cohesive society requires a shared philosophical framework which reminds its members that virtues and values are more important and satisfying than the accumulation of wealth or power. In the United States, that framework is rooted in the search for justice and a deep faith in government by and for the people. For the Saudis, Islam provides the central normative force to regulate everyday behavior.

For Muslim men and for Muslim women...
For men who believe and for women who believe...
For men who speak the truth and women who speak the truth...
For men who persevere in righteousness and for women who persevere in righteousness...
For men who are humble and for women who are humble...
For men who give charity and for women who give charity...
For men who guard their modesty and for women who guard their modesty...
For men who praise God and for women who praise God...
For all of them, God has prepared forgiveness and a vast reward.

Qur'an: collection of verses

In other Muslim countries, the purity of the faith was diluted by colonial rule and the intrusion of outsiders, but Saudi Arabia's remoteness and harsh environment assured its isolation until the middle of the 20th century. The hold of Islam on the people remains intact. Today the Saudis' overriding concern is that secular goals and values do not usurp the dominant place of religion in their society.

> And hold fast, all together, by the Rope which God (stretches out for you), and be not divided among yourselves; and remember with gratitude God's favors on you, for ye were enemies and He joined your hearts in love, so that by His Grace ye became brethren; . . .
>
> Let there arise out of you a band of people inviting to all that is good, enjoining what it right, and forbidding what is wrong. They are the ones to attain felicity.
>
> *Qur'an: III, 103-104*

DRAMATIC CHANGE WITHIN THREE DECADES

As a result of the stunning increase in oil revenues since 1970, Saudi Arabia has moved from a timeless pastoral society into the bustle of modernization within three short decades. The first paved road connected Jiddah, Saudi Arabia's foremost commercial port, to Riyadh, the capital, in 1967. Since then, airplanes, study abroad, newspapers, radios, and television have spread new wants and new attitudes. The psychological adjustments implicit in this swift leap forward cannot be absorbed within a single generation.

Only twenty years ago, the predecessors of today's air-conditioned malls were crowded suqs, with narrow, dark shops opening directly onto the street, their proprietors seated on rugs amidst their goods, by the light of kerosene lanterns. In the countryside the Bedouin women no longer laboriously weave black tents of goats' hair; they are captivated now by garishly decorated canvas tents. Their men drive pickup trucks, transporting and pampering their camels for sport racing. The dearth of water in their desert landscape has been relieved by countless wells and 170 dams, put in place in the last two decades. Over 30 desalinization plants on the two coasts ship millions of gallons of fresh water every day so that Saudi Arabia's city dwellers can take showers and run washing machines. The Saudis do not waste time wondering why all this has happened so suddenly. God has been kind to them, and they accept their good fortune as they accept all His blessings. Islam permits innovation and change as long as progress serves the faith and does not contradict its basic tenets.

The experience of the last two decades has taught thoughtful Saudis, however, that their fabulous wealth is not an unmixed blessing. Oil revenues have made the state dependent on foreign markets and an expatriate work force, rather than on the productive capabilities of its citizens. The rate of oil production is increasingly determined by international exigencies rather than domestic needs.

Rather than let every citizen become a ward of the state, the Saudi government sought to provide an adequate standard of living and quality of life, then encourage citizens to make it on their own in a free enterprise economy. Elaborate social services have been provided, with all the expensive infrastructure needed for modernization, and a middle class has been created—with an outlook different from that of the military, bureaucratic, and religious elites who dominated the old order. The traditional elite, however, still controls the political process. Questions inevitably arise as to whose responsibility it is to make the whole mechanism work.

Expatriots have been hired to erect the edifice, but they have been permitted to structure a modern economy according to international standards, which do not always take into account ingrained Saudi attitudes and culture. When the foreigners leave, the Saudis must operate this complicated mechanism by themselves.

The Saudis have had no trouble accepting the machines and gadgets of modern technology, but reverence for traditions focused on religion and family makes it more difficult to adjust to new standards and ways of thinking inherent in modernization—a work ethic, adherence to rigid time schedules, planning and executing the methodology and logistics of change, tending to maintenance and the myriad details of industrialization. Building roads and refineries is easy compared to the task of instilling new motivations and work habits. Those who believe that God determines all outcomes may be uncomfortable with the rationalism needed to run complex organizations.

Saudis who have acquired modern higher education have been gaining experience as they assume responsibility for the operation of their new industries. As more and more of them join the ranks of technocrats, they gradually adopt the skills and attitudes required by sophisticated technology. The second and third generation of Saudi leaders will focus less on the people they know, as did the first generation of university graduates appointed to government positions, and more on the tasks to be done. Family connections may still play a role in professional and commercial success, but a diminishing role. Performance counts more and more.

These new leaders are learning to delegate authority, even when it necessitates surrendering power. They are making difficult decisions, even when a wrong decision can lead to loss of position. When blueprints don't work, or supplies don't arrive, or schedules go by the boards, people on the spot are being held accountable.

The sons of King Abdul Aziz were born between 1902 and 1947, and some of them are still in top leadership positions in the kingdom. They formed their values and perceptions in a world quite different from that in which their sons and grandsons have grown up. Many of the third generation—the grandsons of Abdul Aziz—have places in the top ruling group now, and the time is not far off when the two older generations will pass completely off the scene.

King Abdul Aziz's sons who have followed him to the throne have countered pressures for political liberalization by strengthening ties with the ulama, who resist the idea that man-made legislation could have the authority of sacred law. They have tried to mute material aspirations by emphasizing spiritual restraint. Now, however, King Fahd has institutionalized the rules of government, providing a framework for scrutiny and debate. The next generation and the generation after will have different experiences and expectations on which to base the hard choices that lie ahead.

The survival of the traditional Saudi system will depend, to a large degree, on the continuing flow of oil and wide dispersement of the revenues throughout all segments of the population. The kingdom's petroleum reserves are vast enough to last another century, promising continuing prosperity for many years to come. Its leaders know that peace and stability are absolutely essential to the country's survival. They recognize that the principal threat to stability lies in radical foreign philosophies—either the secular socialism preached by Libya's Qaddafi and Iraq's Saddam Hussein, or the revolutionary theocracy of Iran.

The Politics of Consensus Monarchy

Unlike other Third World countries where those in control of government have sought to monopolize all channels of authority in order to exclude their opponents from power, the Saudi monarchy is rooted in a complex network of relationships that involve all the traditional groups in the kingdom—the ruling family, the ulama, the tribal chiefs. These leaders all know each other and maintain social, political, and economic ties. The House of Saud relies on the cooperation and support of these influential groups.

The network that supports the monarchy is rooted in the many extended families of the peninsula, which still provide social cohesion in Saudi Arabia. Saudis abroad can be as suave and sophisticated as their Western colleagues, but when they are at home in the kingdom, they accept the discipline of their family hierarchy and follow the strict rules that govern family relationships.

Members of the royal family have enjoyed phenomenal wealth, but have not hoarded resource income for themselves while the rest of the population suffered grinding poverty. The wealth has been dispersed and shared at every level, so that very few are hungry or desperately poor. Discontent does not stem from exploitation, but from human nature's tendency to always want more of a good thing. Those who are disgruntled, want, not a piece of the pie (which they already have), but a say in whether the pie is apple or cherry.

Outsiders look at this unusual social cohesion and ask how it can possibly survive in the face of ever- increasing material prosperity. The Saudis scoff at such lack of faith. Saudi citizens can express their grievances, for they are privileged to talk with their leaders face to face in the many private meetings to which they have access. But tradition dictates that such exchanges take place behind closed doors. Public criticism is considered offensive.

Changing Outlook of a Rising Generation of Saudi Leaders

The predominant social phenomenon of the 1980s has been the rapid growth of a new middle class in Saudi Arabia, made up of university graduates. This is a mobile group that has had substantial contact with foreigners, either through travel and study abroad, or by working closely with foreign advisers. They are accustomed to buying and using imports, from air conditioners to disposable diapers.

The monarchy has provided career and business opportunities for all those who earn advanced degrees. Many observers have expected that this new elite would participate increasingly in Saudi affairs, and government has enlisted the support of the educated middle class. Both the technocrats and the princes who appointed them have, however, been forced by the threat of militant fundamentalism to recognize the need for promoting stability ahead of rapid change.

The technocrats are, nevertheless, a potent and growing social force in Saudi Arabia. They began receiving appointments to the Council of Ministers in the 1960s—a healthy trend typified by Minister of Health Ghazi Algosaibi, Minister of Petroleum Zaki Yamani, and Minister of Planning Hishem Nazer, and others. Outside observers assumed that their influence in the decisionmaking process below the level of the senior princes would increase as their numbers did. King Fahd has delegated real authority for the implementation of policy to his ministers, although the making of policy has remained in the hands of his inner circle.

Industrialization and modernization in the West in the 19th century promoted generalized individualism and freedom of thought. An elevated status for successful promoters of commerce and production replaced traditional veneration for inherited status, martial honor, and political domination. The growing middle class in Saudi Arabia is molding a similar evolution.

To date, the system of co-opting educated Saudis into some sort of government activity has succeeded, but has resulted in a huge bureaucracy. Many of the brightest and best recognize this and are already seeking alternatives. Some young graduates choose private enterprise from the beginning. Others often opt for the independent bureaus and public corporations, where the rewards for individual initiative and effort are more visible than in the old bureaucracy.

The economic retrenchment in the 1980s diminished the number of jobs available to new college graduates. Now the growing educated class cannot be so easily absorbed, and many new graduates are having to take jobs in the provinces. The government is emphasizing courses of study tailored to meet the nation's needs rather than the individual's personal preferences.

The vested personal interest of both the middle class and government in evolution toward modernity conflicts with conservative, patrimonial traditions. Pressures for change will come, not from an impoverished peasantry, because the poor are being provided with social services and opportunities for economic betterment almost faster than

they can absorb them, but rather from those elements of Saudi society that are well enough educated to understand the adjustments they
face.

Guest Workers and Their Role in Development

The vast development projects launched in the 1970s required a
substantial expansion of the foreign work force. The number of guest
workers (including dependents) in Saudi Arabia in the mid-1980s was
estimated at more than one-fifth of the total population. Thousands
of Americans and Europeans worked in the petroleum-related and construction industries. Egyptians, Palestinians, Pakistanis, Indians,
Taiwanese, Koreans taught, practiced medicine, filled middle ranks of
business, industry, commerce, and government. Armies of Third World
migrants dug the ditches, collected the garbage, swept the floors, loaded
the lorries. Asian nannies raised the children. For those from Third
World countries, Saudi Arabia offered far more opportunity for
economic betterment than their own overpopulated homelands. Often
the home government of these guest workers became heavily dependent on the hard currency remittances their nationals sent back home.

The workers themselves were handicapped by language and ig-
norance of the labor laws that would protect them from exploitation.
Much of the growing petty crime was blamed on them. If they com-
plained, their hosts could become fearful of political agitation because
these guest workers brought foreign ideas with them, and, perhaps
more important, acted as a highly visible symbol of the foreign role
in the modernization process. Their alien attitudes provided both a
contrast and a challenge to the profoundly conservative Islamic values
and deeply entrenched traditions of Saudi Arabia and contributed to
a growing awareness of the threats implicit in change.

Government leaders were well aware of the dangers of such heavy
reliance on foreigners. Once the nation's infrastructure was largely in
place, a focused policy was adopted in the Third Five Year Plan of
training Saudis to take over vital jobs. The goal was to increase the
Saudi share of the work force from 40.2 percent to 51.2 percent by
doubling enrollment in vocational training programs and expanding
education for women. The number of residence permits issued to
foreigners dropped. Over a million workers were reported to have left
the kingdom after 1985.

The Gulf War further shattered the uneasy cohabitation with the large foreign labor force. When the governments of Yemen and Jordan and the PLO leadership sided with Saddam Hussein, many of those nationals found it wise to leave the kingdom. They will not be allowed to return, and are being replaced by recruits from Pakistan, the Philippines, Taiwan, Korea—any place with trustworthy surplus labor.

Measuring the trustworthiness of foreigners does not, however, solve manpower problems. The kingdom must produce its own managers and technicians, who will assume responsibility for running its modern programs, if it wishes to be free of foreigners. This will take time. Human resource development is a far slower and more intricate process than the building of infrastructure.

The alternative is to keep foreign workers contented by giving them a larger stake in their careers. Highly skilled Arab professionals from neighboring countries who have been filling important advisory posts know that local aspirants are seeking education in ever-increasing numbers, with the intention of replacing them in a few years. These expatriots would prefer to acquire citizenship and own real estate, investing their loyalty in economic security.

INDIVIDUAL VS. COMMUNITY RIGHTS

The Saudi modernization experiment has focused on nourishing and protecting the community rather than on promoting individual rights prized in the West. The Saudi leaders have promoted freedom from want and freedom from fear for all citizens, and have in a large measure succeeded in achieving these. The Saudis believe that Islam is such a perfect religion that freedom of religion is unnecessary. As for the fourth universal human right—freedom of speech—community cohesion takes precedence over alien concepts that could be destabilizing at this stage in the nation's growth.

The official policy of controlling information for public consumption and excluding foreign journalists from Saudi Arabia gives outsiders a distorted view of the kingdom. At the same time, Saudi images of the West are equally distorted. The healthy, positive aspects of democratic aspirations for justice, opportunity, and individual freedom tend to be ignored, while the vices of modernity are often emphasized.

Unmonitored publicity has always been considered a threat in Saudi Arabia; privacy a virtue. Basic decisions are not made in the public forum, but in private meetings. This patterns conforms to Islamic tradition and Arab culture. The Saudi people do not demand or expect freedom of speech, and would mistrust the rash airing of important matters to public scrutiny. Westerners need to understand Saudi sensibilities and not insist on open disclosure of that which is considered private.

Most Saudis want a stable political climate in their country to underpin continued economic and social progress. They hope that Western leaders will not insist on the rapid implementation of unfamiliar measures to expand individual rights. Pressure for premature reform could undermine the present monarchy. The alternative would likely be, not liberal democrats, but militant radicals who might aspire to an even more intolerant and authoritarian dictatorship.

The Saudis would prefer to minimize outside interference, to strive for a peaceful evolution which will permit them to find their own equitable solutions to their problems. Their traditions do not include voting or legislatures or representative government. Any open campaign by outsiders to inject unfamiliar political institutions into Saudi Arabia would risk alienating the Saudis and destroying their kingdom.

SAUDI ARABIA IN AN INTERDEPENDENT WORLD

The world economy today is too interconnected for any nation to exist in isolation, free from outside influences. Saudi Arabia is part of the bridge between the Western world and Asia, with Africa on one side and South Asia on the other. Along its eastern and western borders lie two vital waterways—the Red Sea and the Arabian/Persian Gulf; to the south, the Indian Ocean. All three are of crucial importance in the commercial and strategic routes between East and West.

World Dependence on Trade and Hydrocarbons

Middle Eastern oil will be essential to industrial economies as long as they are dependent on the combustion engine. The 13-member Organization of Petroleum Exporting Countries produces about 40 percent of the world's crude oil. Saudi Arabia has a quarter of all known petroleum reserves. The price of oil is of vital importance to both producers and consumers. Fluctuations in oil prices are dependent on levels of production and stability in the oil-producing regions.

American reliance on Saudi oil has soared. In 1985 the United States purchased 168,000 barrels a day from Saudi Arabia. By 1992 that figure had risen to 1.8 million barrels a day—a tenfold increase. At the same time, Saudi Arabia has nearly doubled its purchases of American goods, and now buys more from the United States than China does.

In spite of public pronouncements about controlling arms sales to the Middle East, defense equipment purchased abroad by Saudi Arabia in the two years following the Gulf War totaled $25 billion. Protection for American jobs led President Bush to approve a $9 billion order for 72 advanced F-15 fighter planes in September 1992. Arguments that these weapons are to box in Iran and Iraq ring somewhat hollow in a region still reeling from the commercial opportunism that permitted Iraq's arms build-up in the 1980s.

Arms transfers to the Middle East as a whole have declined, but are increasing in the oil-rich states of the Gulf. The interests of all concerned might be better served by arms control agreements aimed at establishing a nuclear-free zone in the region, ratification of the 1992 Chemical Weapons Convention and the 1972 Biological Weapons Convention, and publication of an international register of conventional arms transfers to allay fears of suspicious neighbors. Out-of-region political patrons, weapons suppliers, and neutral third parties, prominently the United Nations, should all be involved. Determined pursuit as well of peace negotiations between the Arabs and Israel is absolutely essential to lifting the clouds of anger and mistrust that dominate emotions in the Middle East.

The Saudis muffle criticism of their arms purchases by emphasizing the strength and inflexibility of their radical neighbors and the trauma of Iraq's invasion of Kuwait in 1990. They point to Israel's huge military establishment and the Israeli refusal to sign the nuclear non-proliferation treaty.

Saudi Arabia shares Washington's desire to promote stability in the Gulf. The Saudi government has for years invested heavily in U. S. Treasury bonds. Saudi private investors have also poured capital into the West. In 1992 they bought significant stakes in Citicorp and

Figure 10.

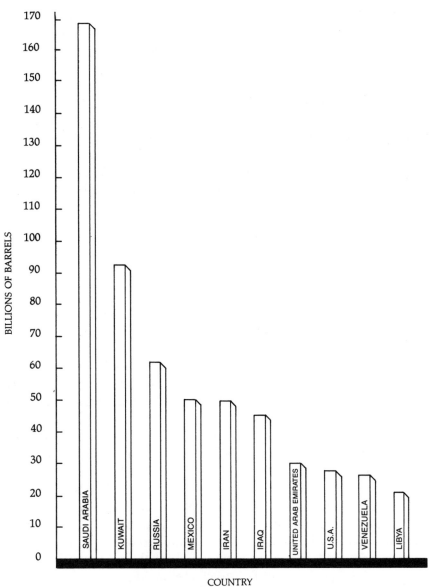

PROVEN OIL RESERVES FOR TOP TEN NATIONS OF THE WORLD

Source: *The World Almanac and Book of Facts 1992.*

Chase Manhattan, two of America's biggest banking companies, and acquired United Press International, an American news service. At the same time, thousands of American businessmen have gone to Saudi Arabia in the last two decades to participate in the vast development programs and the huge profits to be made in the kingdom. Many very reputable American firms have substantial interests there.

The sums of money involved in two-way investment between the kingdom and Western nations are large enough to affect the health of the international business community. This new mutually dependent relationship, reinforced by strategic security interests, should encourage the search for joint strategies to stabilize the Middle East in the post-Cold War world.

Fear of Fundamentalism

The United States has a continuing fear of militant religious leaders who are anti-American and anti-Western. These apprehensions stem from political, rather than religious concerns, for religious labels do not clearly define friends or enemies. Fundamentalist Christians insist on the literal inerrancy of the Bible, but Muslim fundamentalists seek to eliminate secular laws and values and return to the laws and principles of their faith. Religious extremists who are strongly anti-Western are reacting to the failure of alien philosophies—to Western customs, laws, and institutions imposed on their societies by rulers (whether radical dictators or traditional autocrats) who are unable to satisfy popular aspirations.

The revolution in Iran began an era when rulers in Muslim countries cannot openly espouse secular government and dependence on the West without rousing fervent religious opposition. The success of the ayatollahs, who replaced a secular monarch with a theocracy, inspires many militants in the region to claim the sanction of Islam for their political goals. Radicals attract a following among those who resent existing governments and the gap between the rich and the poor.

The material, economic, and technological accomplishments of the West give it overwhelming power, yet Muslims are confident that their spiritual values are superior. Their militancy rises from frustration when they are unable to resist imitating the West. They believe that their feelings of inadequacy will be erased, not by adopting Western institutions such as elections and parliaments, but by returning to a purer form of Islam.

Militant Muslims in turn exploit local secular ambitions, fears, and interests for their own ends. Anti-American sentiment in Iran stemmed from United States support for Shah Muhammad Reza Pahlavi. The Ayatollah Khomeini called America the great Satan, portraying American culture as a "whispering evil"—an enticement away from Muslim values. The Prophet Muhammad spoke of beneficent angels and good spirits, and warned against the influence of the devil and evil spirits. The success of the religious revolution that deposed the shah in Iran and condemned the United States as his sponsor provided a rousing model for other extremist groups throughout the Middle East to emulate. Even Saddam Hussein proclaimed the faith once he was embroiled in Desert Storm.

Say: I seek refuge with the Lord and Cherisher of Mankind, the King (or Ruler) of Mankind, the God (or Judge) or Mankind, from the mischief of the Whisperer (of evil) who withdraws (after his whisper,—(the same) who whispers into the hearts of Mankind,—among Jinns and among Men.

Qur'an: CXIV, 1-6

Governments where Islam is the official religion find it difficult to punish their citizens for rallying behind Muslim banners. When nervous regimes do impose restrictions on political expression, dissenters turn to the mosques as their forum. Egypt, Jordan and Syria are constantly trying to constrain their Muslim Brotherhoods. A new group of Palestinians called Hamas, formed in 1987 to back the *intifada* in the occupied territories controlled by Israel, now has widespread support. Islamic parties in Algeria threaten the governments of Tunisia and Morocco.

Islamic fundamentalism is not, however, automatically anti-Western. Saudi Arabia's Muslim rulers have never been anti-American or threatened the United States' strategic interests. Although they consider themselves superior to Americans in the spiritual realm, they have adopted Western technology, social services, and mass benefits, and these are the yardstick by which they are measuring progress.

New Expectations Following the End of the Cold War

King Fahd spoke as follows to the 10th Summit of the Non-Aligned Movement in 1992: "The stunning developments in international relations over the last few years brought an end to the Cold War. The world has ever since witnessed signs of an emerging international order based on cooperation in lieu of confrontation, and guided by the principles of the United Nations and international legality which reject the use of force and call for negotiation and peaceful means for the settlement of disputes.

"We have to concentrate on the aspects of a fruitful cooperation between the North and South and to give more emphasis to social and economic development, especially since the majority of our membership suffer from the problems of poverty and underdevelopment."

The king went on to reiterate Saudi Arabia's support for a just settlement of the Palestinian problem, as well as an end to Serbian aggression in Bosnia-Herzegovina and national reconciliation in Somalia (where the kingdom has sent substantial emergency relief)—both countries where Muslims are dying in large numbers. Saudi Arabia's pervasive Islamic heritage dictates its concern for Muslim populations, be they in Europe or Asia.

The king also called for the expansion of world trade. "To this end, it is essential that developed countries cooperate in opening their markets for developing countries' products, dismantle protectionist measures, promptly and successfully conclude the Uruguay Round of GATT, and formulate urgent solutions to the problem of indebtedness. Economic cooperation among developing countries is equally essential and represents an important instrument to foster economic development."

These are the words of an internationalist, of a leader who seeks cooperation, rather than confrontation. The Saudis know that future peace and prosperity depend on the promotion of harmonious relations around the world. They are very aware of the crucial importance of petroleum in 20th century economies and the pivotal role Saudi Arabia plays in world politics.

The Saudis look back with pride to the glory of the Muslim Empire in the 9th and 10th centuries, when Arabs banners flew over every town from the Atlantic to the Indus, and Arab learning and culture dominated the Mediterranean. They dream of another flowering of

Arab genius. Today's oil prosperity seems to make almost anything possible. The Saudis speak of *nahda*, which means "rebirth." They see no reason why God's gifts cannot lead again to prosperity and accomplishments that replicate that earlier Golden Age.

If an Arabian renaissance does materialize, it may well result from an amalgamation of Western technology and Muslim values, in much the same way that a fusion of cultures produced dynamism for that glorious Muslim Empire. The challenge is, of course, for the Saudis to shape a destiny that matches their aspirations, blending the best of both worlds into their own unique culture.

Saudi Architects designing the future.

Modern education for the younger generation.

Students from King Fahd University of Petroleum and Minerals.

Saudi farmers grow substantial amounts of grains such as corn, barley, sorghum, and millet.

Saudi Arabia occupies a leading position in world date production.

Al-Hasa water project where hundreds of miles of concrete irrigation and drainage channels web across 50,000 acres.

SELECTED BIBLIOGRAPHY

Al-Farsy, Fouad. *Modernity and Tradition: The Saudi Equation.* London: Kegan Paul International, 1990.

Al-Suhrawardy, Allama Sir Abdullah Al-Mamun. *The Sayings of Muhammed.* New York: Citadel Press, 1938.

Al-Sweel, Dr. Abdulaziz and J.W. Wright, Jr. *Saudi Arabia: Tradition and Transition.* Hayden-McNeil Publishing, Inc. 1993.

Azzam, Henry T. *The Gulf Economies in Transition.* New York: St. Martin's Press, 1988.

Holy Qur'an.

Heller, Mark and Nadav Safran. *The New Middle Class and Regime Stability in Saudi Arabia.* Cambridge, MA: Center for Middle Eastern Studies, Harvard University, 1985.

Islam, A Global Civilization. Royal Embassy of Saudi Arabia, 1990.

Ministry of Finance and National Economy, Economist Intelligence Unit, Saudi Arabia Country Profile, 1992-1993.

Ministry of Planning, *Third Development Plan 1980-1985; Fourth Development Plan, 1985-1990; Fifth Development Plan 1990-1995.*

Ministry of Information, Saudi Arabian National Archives.

OPEC Annual Statistical Bulletin. 1990; Saudi ARAMCO Annual Report, 1990.

Rashid, Dr. Nasser Ibrahim, and Dr. Esber Ibrahim Shaheen. *Christian Science Monitor, Saudi Arabia and the Gulf War, May 15, 1990*

Schimmel, Annemarie. *Islam.* Albany: State University of New York Press, 1992.

The Washington Report on Middle East Affairs, November 1992.

The World Almanac and Book of Facts, 1992.

Recent Dissertations and Theses by Saudi Scholars

Abahusain, Nawal A., "Differences in Parents' Child Rearing Practices and the Sociometric Status of Their Children." (Sociology) M.A. thesis. Colorado State University. 1989. #02727.

Abdulkader, Ahmed Mohammed, "Economic Feasibility of Greenhouse Vegetation Production in. . ." (Agricultural Economics) M.Sc. thesis. 1992. #3023.

Abdulwahid, Abdulrahaman, "Communication and National Security." (Communication) Ph.D. dissertation. Fletcher School of Law. 1988. #02214.

Akeel, Suleiman Abdullah, "The Impact of Modernization on Saudi Society." (Sociology) Ph.D. dissertation. 1992. #2987.

Aklobi, Fahad Abdullah M., "A Survey of Attitudes of Social Studies Teachers and. . ." (Education, Curriculum) Ph.D. 1992. #3007.

Ammari, Abdullah Saad, "Climatic and Geologic Influences on the Hydrology of al-Kharj. . ." (Geography) M.Sc. thesis. 1991. #3053.

Askar, Mohammad Hussain, "Alliance Formation and Political Fragmentation in the Arab World." (Political Science) Ph.D. dissertation. 1992. #3110.

Awad, Mohammad Hussain, "The Intercultural Transfer of Planning Technology: The Case of Islam and the West." (Sociology) Ph.D. dissertation. University of Southern California. 1990. #02974.

Baz, Rashid Saad, "Patient Satisfaction with Primary Health, Services in Saudi Arabia." (Health Administration) Ph.D. dissertation. 1992. #3130.

Braithen, Mohammed Ibrahim, "Municipal Water Demand Management for Riyadh City, Saudi Arabia." (Geology) Ph.D. dissertation. 1993.#3204.

Dosari, Hamad Shabieb, "A Sociolinguistics Study of Attitudes of Muslim Students,. . ." (Education, Curriculum) Ph.D. dissertation. 1992. #3071.

Faiz, Abdulwahab Mohammed, "A Field Study of How Employees in Multicultural Organization. . ." (Communication) M.A. thesis. 1993. #3196.

Fauzan, Abdallah Mohammed, "The Impact of American Culture on the Attitudes of Saudi Arabian. . ." (Sociology) Ph.D. dissertation. 1992. #2996.

Freith, Mohamed A., "The Historical Background of the Emergence of Muhammad Ibn Abd Al-Wahhab and His Movement." (History) Ph.D. dissertation. University of California, Los Angeles. 1990. #02943.

Gahtani, Saeed Abdullah, "An Overview of the Saudi Arabian Telecommunications System." (Communication) M.Sc. thesis. 1990. #3123.

Ghamdi, Ghazi, "Cultural Center, Dammam in Kingdom of Saudi Arabia." (Architecture) M.Sc. thesis. Illinois Inst. of Technology, 1989. #02570.

Goaib, Saad Mosfer, "A Policy of the New Social Program in the Public School System of Saudi Arabia." (Sociology) Ph.D. dissertation. University of Pittsburgh. 1990. #01612.

Habib, Abdul Rahman Ibrahim, "An Analysis of T.V. News in Three Arab Countries Egypt, Saudi Arabia, and Tunisia" (Communication) Ph.D. dissertation. 1993. #3223.

Habib, Mishaal Sulaiman, "Water Utilization in Riyadh, Saudi Arabia." (Geography)

M.Sc. thesis. 1991. #3043.

Hamad, Saud Ahmad, "A Comparative Study of American and Islamic Criminal Homicide Laws." (Law & Juridical Science) M.A. thesis. University of Kansas. 1990. #02767.

Hamdan, Saeed Saeed, "Social Change in the Saudi Family." (Sociology) Ph.D. dissertation. Iowa State University. 1990. #02168.

Haqeel, Abdullah Saleh O., "Experimental and Numerical Study of a Doubly Diffuse Flow." (Communication) Ph.D. dissertation. 1993. #3194.

Hazzaa, Abdulaziz Mohammad, "Women's Education and Work in Saudi Arabia." (Sociology) M.A. thesis. University of Minnesota. 1990. #02956.

Heezan, Mohammad Abdulaziz, "Comparative Analysis of Audience Exposure to the First Channel." (Communication) Ph.D. dissertation. 1993. #3209.

Jarbou, Ayoub Mansour Ali, "Hisbah in Islam, and Its Practice in Saudi Arabia." (Law) LL.M. 1992. #3076.

Jasir, Abdullah Saad H., "Social, Cultural and Academic Factors Associated with Adjustment of Saudi..." (Sociology) Ph.D. dissertation. 1993. #3197

Jomaih, Ibrahim A., "The Use of the Qur'an in Political Argument: A Study of Early Islamic Parties (35-86 A.H./656-705 A.D.)." (History) Ph.D. dissertation. University of California, Los Angeles. 1988. #02188.

Kahtany, Abdullah H., "Anaphoric Relations in Arabic and English Spoken Narratives." (Linguistics) Ph.D. dissertation. 1992. #3019.

Khathllan, Saleh Mohammed Farhan, "Uzbeks and Islam: Their Contemporary Political Culture an Empirical..." (Political Science) Ph.D. dissertation. 1993. #3195.

Maajeeny, Osama Hassan, "Gifted and Talented Learners in the Saudi Arabian Regular Classroom." (Education, Curriculum) Ph.D. dissertation. 1990. #3258, UMI.

Makinsky, Adel AbdulQadir, "The Effects of Mass Communication on Saudi Arabian Students..." (Communication) M.A. thesis. 1991. #3020.

Malki, Sadig Abdul-Hameed, "Institutional Inconsistency: A New Perspective of the Role..." (Political Science) Ph.D. dissertation. 1991. #3126.

Manghlooth, Fahad Hamed, "A Study of Social Work in Community Development Practice in Saudi Arabia." (Sociology) Ph.D. dissertation. 1992. #3112.

Mansour, Ibrahim Mohammed, "Structural Determinants of Political Democracy: A Cross National Study." (Political Science) Ph.D. dissertation. 1993. #3322.

Mennaa, Fahad Nasser, "Islam and the Nature of Law Case Study: Saudi Arabia." (Criminal Justice) M.A. thesis. 1991. #2994.

Merdad, Adel Siraj Saleh, "Foreign TV Programs and Their Sources: An Empirical Analysis." (Communication) Ph.D. dissertation. 1993. #3319

Mobarak, Nasser A., "Cultural Center, Jeddah in Kingdom of Saudi Arabia." (Architecture) M.S. thesis. Illinois Inst. of Technology. 1988. #02125.

Motairi, Thamir Malooh A., "Role of Top-Level Executive Leaders..." (Public Administration) Ph.D. dissertation. 1992. #3088.

Mtairi, Naief Moneef, "The Development Process and Its Relation to Oil Revenues and..." (Sociology) Ph.D. dissertation. 1991. #3057.

Mulhim, Mohammed Ali, "Urban Morphological Changes in Hofuf, Saudi Arabia." (Geography) Ph.D. dissertation. 1993. #3332.

Nafjan, Fahad Mohammed, "The Origins of Saudi-American Relations: From Recognition to Diplomatic Representation (1931-1943)." (History) Ph.D. dissertation. University of Kansas. 1989. #02648.

Otaiby, Abdullah A. "Migration and Socioeconomic Development." (Sociology) Ph.D. dissertation. 1989. #3266. UMI.

Qahtani, Salem Ali Salem, "The Impact of National/International Contemporary Events On. . ." (Education, Curriculum) Ph.D. dissertation. 1992. #2988.

Saaran, Saad Abdulaziz N., "State and Agriculture in Saudi Arabia," (Sociology) Ph.D. dissertation. 1992. #2991.

Sakran, Muhamad Suliman, "A Theoretical Perspective for Explaining Factors Associated with. . ." (Sociology) Ph.D. dissertation. 1992. #3132.

Samergandi, Rogayah Shokrallah, "A Study of Factors that Contribute to the Discrepancy Between. . ." (Sociology) Ph.D. dissertation. 1992. #3105

Al-Saud, Abdullah F., "The Saudi Audience and Television News: An Empirical Analysis of the Saudi News Audience Activity and Involvement with Newscasts in the Saudi Television First Channel." (Communication) M.A. thesis. Michigan State University. 1989. #02530.

Sehaim, Saleh Abdullah, "The Saudi Industrial Development Fund: Impact in Developing the. . ." (Public Administration) Ph.D. dissertation. 1989. #3302, UMI.

Shabanah, Torki Abdullah Mohammed, "Urban Morphological Changes in Hofuf, Saudi Arabia: Impact of Western. . ." (Law) M.A. thesis. 1992. #3331.

Shahrani, Abdullah S., "Modernization in a Traditional Society: The Case of Saudi Arabia." (Sociology) Ph.D. dissertation. Atlanta University. 1990. #02765.

Sowayel, Naila, "An Empirical Analysis of Saudi Arabia's Foreign Policy In. . . (History) Ph.D. dissertation. 1990. #3304, UMI.

Zahrani, Saad Said A., "Cross-Cultural Differences in Attributions of Responsibility to the Self, the Family, the Ingroup and the Outgroup in the U.S.A. and Saudi Arabia: Western Versus Non-Western Cultural. . ." (Sociology) Ph.D. dissertation. Michigan State University. 1991. #00906.

Zarah, Sawsan Mohammed, "Past and Future Research on Higher Education in Saudi Arabia." (Education, Higher) Ph.D. dissertation. 1991. #3075.

Saudi Arabia: A Kingdom In Transition
Books on Saudi Arabia

Belling, Willard A., ed. *King Faisal and the Modernization of Saudi Arabia.* Boulder, CO. Westview Press, 1980.

Clements, Frank A. *Saudi Arabia.* Oxford, England: Clio Press, 1979.

Cleron, Jean Paul. *Saudi Arabia 2000.* New York: St. Michaels Press, 1978.

Crane, Robert. *Planning the Future of Saudi Arabia: A Model for Achieving National Priorities.* New York: Praeger Publishers, 1978.

Dahlen, Ahmed Hassan, ed. *Politics, Administration & Development in Saudi Arabia.* Brentwood, MD: Amana Corporation, 1990.

Helms, Christine Moss. *The Cohesion of Saudi Arabia: Evolution of Political Identity.* Baltimore: Johns Hopkins University Press, 1970.

Holden, David & Johns, Richard. *The House of Saud: The Rise and Rule of the Most Powerful Dynasty in the Arab World.* New York: Holt, Rinehard & Winston, 1981.

Nibloch, Tim, ed. *State, Society & Economy in Saudi Arabia.* London: Croom Helm, 1982.

Nicholson, Eleanor. *In the Footsteps of the Camel: A Portrait of the Bedouins of Eastern Saudi Arabia in Mid-Century.* London: Stacey International, 1983.

Nyrop, Richard F., ed. *Saudi Arabia: Country Study.* Washington, D.C.: U.S. Department of the Army, 1984.

Scholfield, Daniel, editor in chief. *The Kingdom of Saudi Arabia.* Atlantic Highlands, NJ: Stacey International, 1986.

Trueller, Gary. *The Birth of Saudi Arabia: Britain and the Rise of the House of Saud.* London: Frank Cass & Company LTD., 1976.

Winder, R. Bayley. *Saudi Arabia in the Nineteenth Century.* New York: St. Martin's Press, 1985.

Appendix A

THE BASIC LAW OF GOVERNMENT

Chapter One: General Principles

Article 1. The Kingdom of Saudi Arabia is a sovereign Arab Islamic state with Islam as its religion; God's Book and the Sunna of his Prophet, God's prayers and peace be upon him, are its Constitution; Arabic is its language; and Riyadh is its capital.

Article 2. The State's public holidays are 'Id al-Fitr and 'Id al- Adha. Its calendar is the hegira calendar.

Article 3. The State's flag shall be as follows:
a. It shall be green.

b. Its width shall be equal to two thirds of its length.

c. The words "There Is No God But Allah, and Muhammad Is Allah's Prophet" shall be inscribed in its center with a drawn sword under it. The statute shall define the rules pertaining to it.

Article 4. The State's emblem shall consist of two crossed swords with a palm tree in the upper space between them. The statute shall define the State's anthem and its medals.

Chapter Two: Law of Government

Article 5.
a. The law of government in the Kingdom of Saudi Arabia is Monarchy.

b. Rule passes to the sons of the founder King 'Abd-al-'Aziz Bin 'Abd-al-Rahman al-Faysal al Sa'ud and to their children's children. The most upright among them is to be paid allegiance in accordance with (the principles of) the Holy Koran and the Venerable Prophet's Tradition.

c. The king chooses the heir apparent or relieves him by royal order.

d. The heir apparent is to devote his time as an heir apparent and to whatever missions the king entrusts him with.

e. The heir apparent assumes the powers of the king on the latter's death until the act of allegiance has been carried out.

Article 6. Citizens are to pay allegiance to the king in accordance with the Holy Koran and the Prophet's Tradition, in submission and obedience and in times of ease and difficulty, fortune, and adversity.

Article 7. The Government of the Kingdom of Saudi Arabia derives power from the Holy Koran and the Prophet's Tradition.

Article 8. The Government of the Kingdom of Saudi Arabia stands on the bases of justice, shura (consultation), and equality, in accordance with the Islamic shari'ah.

Chapter Three: Constituents of the Saudi Family

Article 9. The family is the kernel of Saudi society . . . and its members shall be brought up on the basis of the Islamic faith, and the loyalty and obedience to God, His messenger, and to guardians . . . respect for and implementation of the law, love of and pride in the homeland, and the glorious history that the Islamic faith stipulates.

Article 10. The State will aspire to strengthen family ties, maintain its Arab and Islamic values, and care for all its members, and to provide proper conditions for the growth of their resources and capabilities.

Article 11. Saudi society will be based on the principle of adherence to God's bond, on its cooperation in good deeds and piety, and on vouching for each other and on their indivisibility.

Article 12. The consolidation of national unity is a duty, and the state will prevent anything that may lead to disunity, sedition or separation.

Article 13. Education will aim at instilling the Islamic faith in the young generation, to provide them with knowledge and skills, and to prepare them to become useful members in the building of their society, members who love their homeland and are proud of its history.

Chapter Four: Economic Principles

Article 14. All God's bestowed wealth, be it underground, on the surface, or in national territorial waters, on the land, or in maritime domains under the State's control, all such wealth resources are the property of the State as defined by the law. The law defines means of exploiting, protecting and developing such wealth in the interest of the State, its security, and its economy.

Article 15. No privilege is to be granted and no public resource is to be exploited without a law.

Article 16. Public funds are sacrosanct. The State has an obligation to protect them, and both citizens and residents are.to preserve them.

Article 17. Property, capital, and labor are essential elements in the Kingdom's economic and social being. They are personal rights which perform a social function in accordance with the Islamic shari'ah.

Article 18. The State protects the freedom of private property and its sanctity. No one is to be stripped of his property except when this serves public interest, in which case fair compensation is due.

Article 19. The public confiscation of money is prohibited and the penalty of the private confiscation is to be imposed only by a legal order.

Article 20. Taxes and fees are to be imposed on the basis of justice and only when the need for them arises. The imposition, amendment, revocation of, and exemption from them is only permitted by law.

Article 21. Tithes (al-zakatu) are to be levied and paid to legitimate recipients.

Article 22. Economic and social development is to be achieved according to a just and scientific plan.

Chapter 5: Rights and Duties

Article 23. The State protect Islam; it implements it's shari'ah; it orders people to do right and to shun evil; it fulfills the duty regarding God's call.

Article 24. The State works to build and serve the holy places; it provides security and care for those who come on pilgrimage and minor pilgrimage by providing facilities and peace.

Article 25. The State strives to attain the hopes of the Arab and Islamic nation for solidarity and unity of word, and to consolidate its relations with friendly States.

Article 26. The State protects human rights in accordance with the Islamic shari'ah.

Article 27. The State guarantees the right of the citizen and his family in cases of emergency, illness, disability, and old age. It supports the system of social security and encourages institutions and persons to contribute acts of charity.

Article 28. The State provides job opportunities to whoever is capable of carrying out such jobs; it enacts laws that protect the employee and the employer.

Article 29. The State guards science, literature and culture; it encourages scientific research; it protects the Islamic and Arab heritage and contributed to Arab, Islamic, and human civilization.

Article 30. The State provides public education and pledges to combat literacy.

Article 31. The State takes care of health issues and provides health care for each citizen.

Article 32. The State works for the preservation, protection, and improvement of the environment and for the prevention of pollution.

Article 33. The State establishes and equips the armed forces for the defense of the Islamic religion, the two holy places, society and the citizen.

Article 34. The defense of the Islamic religion, society, and the country is the duty of each citizen. The regime explains the provision of the military service.

Article 35. The statutes shall define the regulations governing Saudi Arabian nationality.

Article 36. The State shall provide security for all its citizens and all residents within its territory, and no one shall be arrested, imprisoned, or have his actions restricted except in accordance with the provisions of the law.

Article 37. Houses shall have their sanctity and shall not be entered without the permission of their owners or be searched except in cases specified by statutes.

Article 38. Penalties shall be personal and there shall be no crime or penalty except in accordance with religious law (shari'ah) or organizational law (nizami). There shall be no punishment except for acts committed subsequent to the coming into force of the organizational law.

Article 39. Information, publications, and all expression media shall adhere to courteous language (kalimah tayyibah) and the State's regulations and shall contribute to educating the nation and bolstering its unity. All acts that lead to sedition or division or harm the State's security and its public relations or detract from man's dignity and rights shall be prohibited. The statutes shall define all that.

Article 40. Telegraphic, postal, telephonic, and other means of communication messages shall be safeguarded. They can not be confiscated, delayed, read, or listened to except in cases defined by statutes.

Article 41. Residents in the Kingdom of Saudi Arabia shall abide by its laws and shall observe the values of Saudi society and shall respect its traditions and sentiments.

Article 42. The State shall grant political asylum when public interest demands this. The statutes and international agreements shall define the law and procedures governing the extradition of ordinary criminals.

Article 43. The king's court and that of the crown prince shall be open to all citizens and to anyone who has a complaint or a plea against an injustice. Every individual shall have the right to address the public authorities in all matters affecting him.

Chapter Six: Authorities of the State

Article 44. The Authorities of the State consist of the following:
a. The judicial authority
b. The executive authority
c. The regulatory authority

These authorities will cooperate with each other in the performance of their duties in accordance with this and other laws. The king shall be the point of reference for all these authorities.

Article 45. The source of the deliverance of fatwa in the Kingdom of Saudi Arabia...are God's Book and the Sunna of his messengerThe law will define the composition of the senior ulema body, the administration of scientific research, the deliverance of fatwa, and the body of the senior ulema's functions.

Article 46. The judiciary is an independent authority...there is no hegemony over judges in the dispensation of their judgment except for that of the Islamic shari'ah.

Article 47. The right to litigate is ensured for citizens and residents in the Kingdom on an equal basis. The law defines the required procedures for this.

Article 48. The courts will apply the rules of the Islamic shari'ah to the cases that are brought before them, in accordance with what is indicated in the Book and the Sunna, and the statutes decreed by the ruler which do not contradict the Book or the Sunna.

Article 49. By observing what is stated in Article 53 of this law, courts shall arbitrate in all disputes and crimes.

Article 50. The king or whoever deputizes for him, is concerned with implementing judicial rulings.

Article 51. The system explains the formation of the Higher Council of Justice and prerogatives; it also explains the ranking lists of the courts and their prerogatives.

Article 52. The appointment of judges and the termination of their duties are carried out by a royal decree, according to a proposal from the Higher Council of Justice, in accordance with the provisions of the law.

Article 53. The law explains the ranking lists of the tribunal of complaints and its prerogatives.

Article 54. The law explains the relation between the body of investigation and the general prosecutor, and their organization and prerogatives.

Article 55. The king carries out the policy of the nation, a legitimate policy in accordance with the provisions of Islam; the king oversees the implementation of the Islamic shari'ah, the systems, the State's general policies, and the protection and defense of the country.

Article 56. The king is the head of the Council of Ministers; he is assisted in carrying out his duties by members of the Council of Ministers in accordance with the provisions of this law and other laws. The system of the Council of Ministers explains the prerogatives of the Council concerning domestic and foreign affairs, and the organization of, and coordination between, government apparatuses. It also explains the conditions that should be fulfilled by the ministers, their prerogatives, the system of their questioning, and all their issues. The law of the Council of Ministers and its prerogatives are to be amended in accordance with this law.

Article 57.

a. The king appoints and relieves deputies of the prime minister and members of the Council of Ministers by royal decree.

b. The deputies of the prime minister and ministers of the Council of Ministers are considered responsible, by expressing solidarity to the king, for implementing the Islamic shari'ah and the State's general policy.

c. The king has the right to dissolve and reorganize the Council of Ministers.

Article 58. The king appoints those who enjoy the rank of ministers, deputy ministers and an excellent class, and relieves them from their posts by a royal decree in accordance with explanations included in the law. The ministers and head of independent departments are responsible, before the prime minister, for the ministries and departments that they supervise.

Article 59. The law defines the rules of the civil service, including salaries, awards, compensation, favors, and pensions.

Article 60. The king is commander-in-chief of all the armed forces. He appoints officers and ends their service according to the law.

Article 61. The king declares a state of emergency, general mobilization, and war; and the law defines the rules of this.

Article 62. If there is danger that threatens the safety of the Kingdom or its territorial integrity, or the security of its people and its interests, or that impedes the functioning of State institutions, the king may take urgent measures to face this danger. And, if the king sees that these measures should continue, he may then adopt the necessary regulations to this end.

Article 63. The king receives kings and heads of state. He appoints has representatives to States, and he receives the credentials of State representatives to him.

Article 64. The king awards medals as defined by regulations.

Article 65. The king may delegate prerogatives to the crown prince by royal decree.

Article 66. In the event of travel abroad, the king issues a royal decree delegating to the crown prince the management of the state's affairs and the looking after of the interests of the people, as defined by the royal decree.

Article 67. The regulatory authority lays down regulations and motions likely to meet the interests of, or remove what is bad in, the affairs of the State, in accordance with the Islamic shari'ah. This authority exercises its functions in accordance with this law and the laws pertaining to the Council of Ministers and the Shura Council.

Article 68. A Consultative Council is to be created. Its statute will show how it is formed, how it exercises its powers, and how its members are selected. The king has the right to dissolve the Consultative Council and to reform it.

Article 69. The king has the right to call the Consultative Council and the Council of Ministers to convene a joint meeting and to invite whomever he wishes to attend that meeting to discuss whatever matter he wishes.

Article 70. International treaties, agreements, regulations, and concessions are approved and amended by royal decrees.

Article 71. Statutes are to be published in the official gazette and take effect from the date of publication, unless another date is specified.

Chapter Seven: Financial Affairs

Article 72.
a. The statute explains the provisions of the State's earnings and their deposit in the State's general budget.
b. Earnings are entered and spent according to rules specified in the statute.

Article 73. Any undertaking to pay a sum of money from the general budget must be made according to the provisions of the budget. If this is not possible according to the provisions of the budget, it will then be done according to a royal decree.

Article 74. Selling, renting, or using State's assets is not permitted except in accordance with the statute.

Article 75. The statutes will define monetary and banking provisions, as well as standards, weights and measures.

Article 76. The law will fix the State's financial year and will announce the budget by way of a royal decree. It will also assess the revenues and expenditures of that year, at least one month before the start of the financial year. If, for necessary reasons, the budget is not announced, and the new financial year starts, the previous years budget will remain in force until the new budget is announced.

Article 77. The competent body will prepare the State's final statement of accounting for the passing year and will submit it to the head of the Council of Ministers.

Article 78. The same provisions will apply to both to the budgets of public corporate bodies and their final statements of accounting and to the State's budget and its final statement of accounting.

Chapter Eight: Control Bodies

Article 79. All the State's revenues and expenditures will be under subsequent control, and all the State's liquid and nonliquid funds will be controlled to ascertain the good use of these funds and their preservation. An annual report will be submitted on the matter to the head of the Council of Ministers. The law will define the competent control body and its obligations and prerogatives.

Article 80. The government bodies will be under control to ascertain the good performance of the administration and the implementation of the statutes. Financial and administrative offenses will be investigated, and an annual report will be submitted on the matter to the head of the Council of Ministers. The law will define the competent body in charge of this and its obligations and prerogatives.

Chapter Nine: General Provisions

Article 81. The implementation of this law will not prejudice the treaties and agreements signed by the Kingdom of Saudi Arabia with international bodies and organizations.

Article 82. Without violating the contents of Article 7 of this law, no provision of this law whatsoever can be suspended unless it is temporary, such as in a period of war or during the declaration of a state of emergency. This will be in accordance with the terms of the law.

Article 83. This law will be amended only in the same way it was announced.

SHURA COUNCIL STATUTE

Article 1. In accordance with the words of Almighty God: "It was by some mercy of God that thou was gentle to them; had you been harsh and hard of heart, they would have scattered from about thee. So pardon them and pray forgiveness for them, and take council with them in the affair; and when thou art resolved, put thy trust in God; for surely God loves those who put their trust." In accordance with the words of Almighty God; "And those who answer their Lord and perform the prayer, their affairs being council between them, and they expend of that We have provided them."

Following the prophet of God, may the prayers and blessings of God be upon him in consulting his companions and in inciting the ummah to engage in consultations, the Shura Council is created. It carries out the tasks entrusted to it in accordance with this statute and the basic law of government, with commitment to the Book of God and the tradition of His prophet, and in maintaining the ties of brotherhood and cooperation in kindness and piety.

Article 2. The Shura Council is founded on adherence to God's bonds and commitment to the sources of Islamic jurisprudence. The council members will be keen to serve the public interest, preserve the unity of the jama'a (religious term meaning group of Muslims), the entity of the State, and the interests of the ummah.

Article 3. The Shura Council is composed of a chairman and sixty members chosen by the king from among scholars and men of knowledge and expertise. Their rights and duties and all their affairs are defined by a royal decree.

Article 4. A member of the Shura Council must meet the following conditions:
a) He must be a Saudi national and reside in Saudi Arabia.
b) He must be known to be good and competent.
c) He must be no less than thirty years old.

Article 5. A member of the Shura Council may submit an application to be relieved of membership on the council to the chairman of the council, and the latter will submit this to the king.

Article 6. If a member of the Shura Council fails to carry out the duties of his work, he should be investigated and tried in accordance with the rules and measures to be issued by royal decree.

Article 7. If the post of a Shura Council member becomes vacant for any reason, the king chooses the person to replace him and issues a royal decree in this connection.

Article 8. A member of the Shura Council is not allowed to use his membership for his own interests.

Article 9. It is not permitted to combine membership of the Shura Council with any other government post or to manage any company unless the king sees fit that there is a need for this.

Article 10. The chairman, his deputy, and the secretary general of the Shura Council are appointed and relieved of their posts by royal decrees; and their salaries, rights, duties, and all issues are defined by royal decree.

Article 11. Before beginning their duties on the Shura Council, the chairman, members, and secretary general of the council shall take the following oath before the king: "I swear by God Almighty to be loyal to my religion, then to my King and my country; I swear not to divulge any State secrets; I swear to protect its interests and its systems, and to carry out my duties with sincerity, integrity, loyalty, and justice."

Article 12. Riyadh is the headquarters of the Shura Council. The council may meet in another place inside of the Kingdom of Saudi Arabia if the king deems this necessary.

Article 13. The period of the Shura Council will be four hegira years, starting from the date specified in the royal decree issued concerning its establishment. A new council will be formed at least two months before the end of its predecessors term. In the event of the term ending before the formation of a new council, the outgoing council will continue to function until a new council is formed. When a new council is formed, new members must be selected whose number must not be less than half of the total number of council members.

Article 14. The king, or whoever deputizes for him will annually deliver a royal speech at the Shura Council on the State's domestic and foreign policies.

Article 15. The Shura Council will express opinions on the general policy of the State referred to it by the Council of Ministers. The Shura Council may do the following in particular:

a) Discuss the general plan of economic and social development, and express opinion regarding it.

b) Study international laws, charters, treaties, agreements, and concessions, and make appropriate suggestions regarding them.

c) Interpret laws.

d) Discuss annual reports submitted by ministries and other government bodies, and make appropriate suggestions regarding them.

Article 16. The Shura Council's meeting will not be regarded as a quorum without the attendance of at least two-thirds of its members, including the chairman, or whoever deputizes for him. Decisions will not be valid unless they are approved by a majority of the council.

Article 17. The decisions of the Shura Council will be submitted to the Chairman of the Council of Ministers, who will refer them to the Council of Ministers for deliberation. If the views of both councils are in agreement, the decisions will be issued with the king's consent; if the views differ, the king has the right to decide what he deems fit.

Article 18. International treaties, agreements, orders, and concessions are issued and amended by royal decrees, after being studied by the Shura Council.

Article 19. The Shura Council forms from among its members, the specialized committees necessary to exercise its jurisdiction. It can form special committees from among its members to discuss any question on its agenda.

Article 20. The committees of the Shura Council may enlist the help of anyone other than members of the council, with the consent of the chairman of the council.

Article 21. The Shura Council has a General Body consisting of the chairman of the council, his two deputies, and the heads of the specialized committees.

Article 22. The chairman of the Shura Council has to submit to the chairman of the

Council of Ministers the request to summon any government official to meetings of the Shura Council when it discusses matters relating to that official's jurisdiction. The official will have the right to debate, but not the right to vote.

Article 23. Every ten members of the Shura Council have the right to propose a new draft law or amendment to an executive law and submit it to the chairman of the Shura Council. The chairman should submit the proposal to the king.

Article 24. The chairman of the Shura Council should submit a request to the prime minister with regard to providing the council with statements and documents, in the possession of the government apparatus, which the council believes necessary to facilitate its work.

Article 25. The chairman of the Shura Council will submit an annual report to the king on its work, in accordance with the council Internal List.

Article 26. Civil service systems apply to the employees of the council's apparatus, unless the Internal List states otherwise.

Article 27. The Shura Council is to be allocated a special budget by the king, which will be spent in accordance with the rules to be issued by royal decree.

Article 28. The Shura Council's financial matters, financial control, and final statement of accounts are to be organized in accordance with special rules to be issued by royal decree.

Article 29. The Internal List of the Shura Council defines the prerogatives of the chairman of the Shura Council, his deputy, the council's secretary general, the council's apparatus, methods of holding its sessions, the management of its work, the work of its committees, and its method of voting. The list also organizes the rules of debate, ethics of responses, and other such matters that may provide restraint and discipline within the council. for it should exercise its prerogatives for the good of the Kingdom and the probity of its people. This list is to be issued by royal decree.

Article 30. The amendment of this law can only be carried out through the method of which it was published.

REGIONS STATUTE

Article 1. This statute is aimed at improving the level of administrative work and development in the regions of the Kingdom. It is also aimed at maintaining security and order and at guaranteeing the rights and liberties of citizens in the framework of the Islamic shari'ah.

Article 2. The regions of the Kingdom and the headquarters of the emirate of each region are organized by royal decree upon the recommendation of the interior minister.

Article 3. Administratively, each region consists of a number of governorates, districts, and centers, created thus after taking into account demographic, geographic, security, and environmental conditions and communications. The governorate is organized by royal decree on the recommendation of the interior minister. The districts and centers are created and linked by a decision from the interior minister upon the recommendation of the emir of the region.

Article 4. Every region shall have an emir with the rank of minister and a deputy of distinguished grade to assist him in his work and to deputize for him in his absence. The emir and his deputy are appointed to and relieved from, their posts by royal decree upon the recommendation of the interior minister.

Article 5. The emir of the region is accountable to the interior minister.

Article 6. The emir and his deputy, before taking up their responsibilities, shall take the following oath before the king: "I swear by Almighty God to be loyal to my religion, and then to my king and my country, not to disclose any State secrets, to protect its interests and laws, and to discharge my duties with honesty, trust, loyalty, and justice."

Article 7. Every Emir will assume the administration of the region in accordance with the general policy of the State, and in accordance with the rules of this statute and other statutes and motions. He must in particular:

a) Maintain security, order, and stability, and take the necessary measures to this end, in accordance with regulations and motions;

b) Carry out judicial judgements after they become final;

c) Guarantee the rights and liberties of individuals, and take no measure that would harm these rights and liberties, except within the limits decided by the judiciary and the law;

d) Work for the social, economic, and urban development of the region;

e) Work for the development of public services in the region and toward promoting them;

f) Administer governorates, districts, and localities; control the work of governors, district directors, and heads of localities; and make sure that they are discharging their duties in a proper manner;

g) Protect the assets and properties of the State, and prevent any transgressions against them;

h) Supervise the State organs and their employees in the region to ensure that they carry out their duties well, with all trust and loyalty, taking into account the ties of the employees of ministries and various services in the region with their competent authorities;

i) Have direct contact with ministers and heads of services; discuss the affairs of the region with them in order to improve the performance of the organs under his authority; and inform the interior minister about this;

j) Present annual reports to the interior minister about the level of performance of public services in the region and other affairs of the region, as defined by the executory motion of this statute.

Article 8. An annual meeting of the emirs of regions is to take place under the chairmanship of the interior minister, to discuss issues related to regions. The interior minister will submit a report on this matter to the president (as received) of the Council of Ministers.

Article 9. A meeting of the governors of the governorates and directors of districts is to take place at least twice a year, under the chairmanship of the emir of the region, to discuss regional matters. The emir will submit a report on this meeting to the interior minister.

Article 10.
a) For each region, at least one under-secretary, is to be appointed with a rank of not less than 14 (as received) in accordance with a decision by the Council of Ministers, based upon a recommendation from the interior minister.
b) Each governorate has a governorate with a rank of not less than 14. He is to be appointed by the president of the Council of Ministers, upon a recommendation from the interior minister. The governorate has an under-secretary whose rank is not less than 12, and who is to be appointed by the interior minister, upon a recommendation from the emir of the region.
c) Each district has a director, whose rank is not less than 8. He is appointed by the interior minister following a recommendation from the emir of the region.
d) Each locality has a chairman, whose rank is not less than 5. He is appointed by the emir of the region upon a recommendation from the governor of the governorate.

Article 11. Emirs of regions, governors of governorates, administrators of districts, and head of localities have to reside within their work area, and they must not leave the domain of their work, except by permission of their immediate superior.

Article 12. Governors of governorates, administrators of districts, and head of localities will assume their duties in the administrative domain of their areas, and within the limits of the authorities vested in them.

Article 13. The governors of governorates must administer their governorates within the limits of the authorities stipulated in article 7, with the exception of what is stated in Clauses (f), (i), and (j). They must monitor the work of the district administrators and heads of localities who are their subordinates, ascertain that they are competent to carry out their duties, and submit regular reports to the emir of the region on efficiency in the performance of public services and other governorate affairs, as defined in the executive bill of this statute.

Article 14. Every ministry and government concern that provides services in the region must appoint a director of its bodies in the region, whose grade must not be lower than 12, who will directly linked to the central body, and who must coordinate with the emir of the region in the area of his work.

Article 15. A council to be called the Council of the Region, and to be based at the headquarters of the region's emirate will be set up in every region.

Article 16. The Council of the Region will consist of:

a) The emir of the region as chairman of the council;

b) The deputy emir of the region as deputy chairman of the council;

c) The commissioner (wakil) of the region and the governors of the governorates;

d) The heads of the government bodies in the region, which will be specified by an order of the chairman of the Council of Ministers, based on the recommendation of the interior minister.

e) Not less than ten people of learning, experience, and competence from the public, who will be appointed by order of the chairman of the Council of Ministers, on the basis of nominations by the emir of the region, with the approval of the interior minister. Their term of membership will be four years, subject to removal.

Article 17. A member of the council must meet the following requirements:

a) Be of Saudi nationality by birth and upbringing,

b) Be of recognized rectitude and competence,

c) Be no younger than thirty,

d) Be a resident of his region.

Article 18. A member is to submit proposals in writing to the chairman of the region's council on matters coming under the council's jurisdiction. The chairman is to include every proposal on the council agenda, with a view toward putting it forward for examination.

Article 19. A member of a region's council cannot attend deliberations of the council, or of its committees, if the topic presented concerns a personal matter, a matter pertaining to another person whose testimony is not accepted, or to a person for whom the member is acting guardian, proxy or a representative.

Article 20. Should the appointed member wish to resign, he is to submit a request to that effect to the interior minister, through the emir of the region concerned. The resignation will not be considered valid until the prime minister has approved it, acting on the recommendation of the interior minister.

Article 21. Outside the cases mentioned in this statute, an appointed member cannot be dismissed during his term, except by order from the prime minister, acting on a recommendation from the interior minister.

Article 22. Should a vacancy arise for any specific reason, a replacement is to be designated within three months of the vacancy. The new member will then fill the vacancy for the rest of his predecessor's period, in accordance with Clause (e) of Article 16 of this law.

Article 23. The regional council is responsible for studying any point which may improve the standard of services in the region. Its prerogatives are particularly as follows:

a) To define the needs of the region and propose their inclusion in the State's development plan;

b) To define the useful projects according to a scale of priorities, and to propose their endorsement in the State's annual budget;

c) The study plans of organizations of the regions' cities and towns, and to follow up their implementation once they are endorsed;

d) To follow up aspects related to the region, vis-a-vis the development plan, while observing balance and coordination in the matter.

Article 24. The regional council will table any proposal involving general useful works related to citizens of the region, and it will encourage the citizens' contributions in this regard. The proposal should be submitted to the interior minister.

Article 25. The regional council is prohibited from looking into any subject outside the scope of its prerogatives as stipulated for it according to this law. Its decisions will be null and void if it exceeds this. The interior minister will issue a decision in this matter.

Article 26. The regional council will hold an ordinary session every three months, at the invitation of the chairman. The chairman may call for an extraordinary meeting if he deems this fit. The session will included the meeting or meetings held following one invitation, and the session may be concluded only after all the points on the agenda have been examined and discussed.

Article 27. Attendance at the meetings of the regional council is considered a function-related duty for member mentioned in Clauses (c) and (d) of Article 16 of this statute. They must attend in person, or have a person attend in lieu of them in the event of their being away from work. As for the members mentioned in Clause (e) of Article 16, the absence of a member from two successive sessions, without an acceptable excuse, is reason for dismissal from the council. In this case, this member must not be reappointed to the council prior to two years from the date of his dismissal.

Article 28. The meetings of the council will only have a quorum if at least two-thirds of the members are present. The council issue its decisions with an absolute majority of votes by members of the council. If the vote is equal then the side with whom the chairman votes wins.

Article 29. The regional council must, if need be, form special committees to examine any decree falling within the scope of its prerogatives. It may enlist the help of experienced people and specialists. It may also invite anyone it likes to attend the council meetings and to take part in the discussion without having the right to vote.

Article 30. The interior minister must summon the council to convene under his chairmanship, at any venue he chooses. The minister also chairs any meeting he attends.

Article 31. The regional council may convene only at the request of its chairman or his deputy, or by order from the interior minister.

Article 32. The chairman of the council must submit a copy of the reports to the interior minister.

Article 33. The chairman of the regional council must inform the ministries and government departments about resolutions concerning them that are passed by the council.

Article 34. The ministries and government departments must comply with the resolutions passed by the regional council, in accordance with the contents of Clauses (a) and (b) of Article 23 of this law. If a ministry or a government department sees fit not to agree with a resolution passed by the regional council on what has been mentioned, they must clarify the reasons for doing so to the regional council. If the regional council is not convinced that the reasons given by the ministry or government department are suitable, it will refer the case to the interior minister, who will then refer it to the chairman of the council of Ministers.

Article 35. Every ministry or department with services in the region will notify the regional council about the projects decided for the region in the budget as soon as it is issued. It will also notify the council about the development plan decided upon for the region.

Article 36. Every minister and head of service may seek the views of the regional council about any subject connected with his jurisdiction in the region. The council must offer its opinion in this regard.

Article 37. Upon the recommendation of the interior minister, the Council of Ministers will decide the rewards for the chairman of the regional council and its members, taking into consideration the costs transportation and residence.

Article 38. The regional council can be dissolved only by a decision from the chairman of the Council of Ministers, upon recommendation from the interior minister. New members should be appointed within three months from the date of dissolution. During the period when the council is dissolved, the members mentioned in Clauses (c) and (d) of Article 16, under the chairmanship of the Emir of the region will exercise the powers of the council.

Article 39. The regional council has a secretariat [residing] in the region's emirate that will undertake the preparation of its agenda, extend invitations at the appropriate times, record the discussions that take place during the meetings, count votes, prepare the minutes of the meetings, draft the decisions, carry out the necessary work to organize the council's meetings, and record its decisions.

Article 40. The interior minister is to issue the necessary bills to implement this statute.

Appendix B

KING FAHD'S ADDRESS TO THE NATION
ON THE NEW LAWS

In the name of God, the merciful, the compassionate. Thanks be to God, the lord of all universe, and prayers and peace be upon the most noble of prophets, our Lord Muhammad, and upon all his family and companions.

Brother citizens: If God intended good to come to some people he would guide them to what is better for them. God bestowed on us countless bounties, and the greatest of them all is that of Islam, because it is the religion to which we adhere and from which we shall not stray. We will be guided and be pleased by it because Almighty God has said this and said the same to His prophet. The facts of history and reality are the best witness to this. Muslims are happy with the Islamic shari'ah because it became their arbiter in their lives and all their affairs.

In modern history the first Saudi state was established, based on Islam, more than two-and-one-half centuries ago when two pious reformists—Imam Muhammad Bin Sa'ud and Shaykh Muhammad Bin 'Abd al-Wahhab, may God have mercy on their souls—agreed on that. This state was established on a clear program of politics, rule, a call for Islam, and sociology. This program is Islam—belief and shari'ah. . . .

The application of this program continued in all subsequent stages as succeeding rulers continued to abide by the Islamic shari'ah. This was by the grace of God who grants such graces to whom He wishes. This continuous upholding of the program of Islam is based on three facts: the fact that the basis of the program of Islam is fixed and is not subject to change or alteration. . . . Also, the fact that the upholding of the program should be continuous. . . . Third, the fact that the rulers of this state should be faithful to their Islam under all circumstances and conditions. . . .

This program could be summed up in establishing the Kingdom of Saudi Arabia on the following foundations:

1. The unification of faith, which makes the people devote worship to God alone, without a partner, and live strongly and honorably.

2. The code of Islam, which preserves the rights and bloods, organizes the relationship between the governor and the governed, controls transactions between members of the community, and safeguards general security.

3. Adopting the Islamic call and spreading it, because calling for God is among the Islamic state's greatest and most important responsibilities.

4. The founding of a suitable "general environment" free of objectionable actions and deviations which helps guide people toward honesty and righteousness; this mission is a responsibility to support right and shun evil.

5. Achieving the "unity" of faith which is the basis of political, social, and geographic unity.

6. Adopting the means of progress and achieving an "overall awakening" which directs the peoples' lives and their livelihood, and looks after their interests in the light of Islam's guidance and its standards.

7. Achieving "shura," which Islam has ordered and praises whoever takes it up, for Islam ranks it among the qualities of the believers.

8. The two holy mosques shall remain chaste for visitors and worshippers—as they were intended by God—far away from all that which hinders the performance of the minor and major pilgrimage and worship in the best way. The Kingdom shall carry out this duty in fulfillment of God's right and to serve the Islamic nation.

9. To defend the faith and the holy shrines, the homeland, the people, and the state.

These are the great bases on which the Kingdom of Saudi Arabia has been established. The development of modern life necessitated the emergence of major rules from this trend during the era of [the late] King 'Abd-al-'Aziz. In view of the evolution of the state and the growth of its duties, King 'Abd al-'Aziz—may God rest his soul— in the year 1373 A.H. (year beginning 10 September 1953) issued his decree forming a Council of Ministers which is in operation to this day, in accordance with its statute issued in the year 1373 A.H. and the amendments which followed. This program is still in force to this day, with God's grace and guidance.

Therefore, the Kingdom of Saudi Arabia has never known what is termed a "constitutional vacuum." The concept of a "constitutional vacuum" from the standpoint of the text is that the state has no guiding principles, or binding bases, or reference sources in the sphere of legislation and in regulating relations. The Kingdom of Saudi Arabia has never witnessed such a phenomenon in its entire history. Throughout its march, it has ruled according to the guiding principles, obliging bases, and the clear fundamentals to which judges, ulema, and all those employed by the state refer. The whole state apparatus currently functions according to statutes which stem from Islamic shari'ah and are regulated by it.

Therefore, the fact is that we are today enacting the following statutes: the basic statute of governing; the statute of the Consultative Council; and the statute for the regions, in new forms. These have not been forced by a vacuum. These three statutes are aimed at strengthening something which exists and which formulates a de facto matter which is in operation. These statutes will be subject to changes and developments according to requirements of the Kingdom's circumstances and interests.

The pillar and source of the basic statute (of government) is the Islamic shari'ah, as this statute has been guided by the Islamic shari'ah in defining the nature, objectives, and the responsibilities of the state and in defining the relationship between the ruler and the ruled, which is founded on brotherhood, exchanging advice, friendship and cooperation.

The relationship between citizens and those who are in charge of their affairs in this country is founded on firm bases and deep-rooted traditions of love, compassion, justice, mutual respect and loyalty stemming from the free and deep-rooted conviction in the hearts of the sons of this country through successive generations. There is no difference between a ruler and one who is ruled; they are all equal before God, and they are all equal in the love of this homeland and their eagerness to preserve its safety, unity, pride, and progress. The one in charge has rights as well as duties, and the relationship between the ruler and the ruled is first and foremost, and in the final analysis, governed by the law of God, as provided in the Holy Book of God and the tradition of His prophet, may the prayers and blessings of God be upon him.

The basis statute of government is inspired by these principles, and it seeks to expand them in the relationship between ruler and ruled, with a commitment to all that has been brought about by our true religion in this respect.

As to the Shura Council statute, it is based on Islam in both name and content, in response to the saying of God Almighty: "And those who responded to God, and performed prayers, and held consultations among themselves, and spent what we have made available to them . . . ." The new statute of the Consultative Council provides for a modernization and development of the existing system through bolstering the council's framework, and means and methods, with more efficiency, organization, and vitality, in order to achieve the desired objectives. The capabilities to be embodied in this council will be carefully chosen in order to be able to contribute to the development of the Kingdom of Saudi Arabia and its progress, taking onto consideration the public interest of the homeland and the citizens. While the Consultative Council undertakes, God willing, the general consultation at a state level, we must not ignore the currently practiced consultations within the state's organs through the specialized councils and committees. These structures ought to be active so that their work will complement that of the general Consultative Council.

The country has recently witnessed tremendous developments in various areas. These development have called for a renewal of the general administrative system in the country. To meet this need and interest, the statue of regions will allow more organized action through an appropriate administrative leap, and will elevate the level of administrative rule in the regions of the Kingdom.

O Compatriots, these statutes have been laid down after a meticulous and patient study carried out by an elite group of learned men of opinion and experience, taking into consideration the distinguished position of the Kingdom on the Islamic scene and its traditions, customs, and its social, cultural, and civilized conditions. Therefore, these statutes spring from our reality, taking into consideration our traditions and customs, and adhering to our true (Islamic) religion.

We are confident that these statutes will, with God's help, assist the state in realizing all that which the Saudi citizen aspires to: good and progress for his homeland and his Arab and Islamic nation. The Saudi citizen is the basic pivot for the advancement and development of his homeland, and we shall not spare any effort in doing everything to ensure his happiness and reassurance.

The world, which is following the development and progress of this country, greatly admires its internal policy, which safeguards the citizen's security and stability, as well as its rational foreign policy, which is keen on establishing relations with other countries, and which contributes to all that which bolsters the pillars of peace in this world. . . .

The governors adhere to the Islamic line, the officials in the government adhere to it, and the people adhere to it in their transactions and life. Islam is a way of life and [there is] no forfeiting of what is in God's Book, what has been confirmed by his Prophet, or what Muslims have unanimously agreed on. Our constitution in the Kingdom is the Book of Gracious God, which is immune from any vanity, and His messenger's sunna [tradition], who does not speak irresponsibly. Whatever we disagree on, we refer it back to these people. They are the arbiters on all statutes issued by the state. . . .

Citizens, with the help of God, we will continue with our Islamic line, cooperating with those who want good for Islam and Muslims, keen to strengthen the religion of God and the call for it; eager to ensure progress for this country, and happiness for its people. We beg Almighty God to bestow on our people and our Arab and Islamic nation all good, righteousness, progress, prosperity, and happiness. Thanks be to God, who bestows everything righteous.

Appendix C

THE RULING LINE OF THE HOUSE OF SA'UD

The Saudi Arabian state has passed through two stages, usually referred to as the first and second Saudi States. The Saudi Arabian government is presently in a what is known as the third Saudi State. This appendix serves to illustrate these three stages. The first stage was initiated by Imam Mohammad bin Saud, who received and united with Sheikh Mohammad bin Abdulwahab. This stage flourished for approximately fifty-five years. The second stage thrived for nearly fourty-seven years. The third, and current stage was instituted by Abdulaziz bin Abdulrahman Al-Saud (King Abdulaziz), the founder of modern Saudi Arabia. His sons have been ruling the country since his death in 1953.

Appendix C is divided into two sections, reflecting the stages mentioned above. Section one lists the dates of birth and death for the rulers of the first and second stages. Section two corresponds to the third Saudi State, beginning with King Abdulaziz and his sons, who actually ruled the Kingdom. Furthermore, this section includes a current list of all the sons of King Abdulaziz.

Section 1. The First and Second Saudi States

Muhammad bin Saud	1745-1764
Abdulaziz bin Muhammad	1764-1803
Saud bin Abdulaziz	1803-1813
Abdullah bin Saud	1813-1819
Turki bin Abdullah	1819-1833
Faisal bin Turki	1833-1865
Abdulrahman bin Faisal	1884-1891

Section 2. The Third Saudi State

King Abdulaziz bin Abdulrahman bin Faisal bin Turki Al-Saud (Founder of present-day Saudi Arabia) 1876-1953

Saud	Faisal	Khalid	Fahad
1902-1969	1904-1975	1912-1982	1921-

King Abdulaziz Al-Saud was the father of thirty-nine other sons. Some of them have passed away.

First name	Dates	Career
Turki	1900-19	Died in Riyadh Spanish Flu epidemic
Saud	1902-69	Born January 1902; proclaimed crown prince September 1932; Viceroy of Nejd 1932-53; proclaimed king November 9, 1953; deposed November 3, 1964; died February 23, 1969.
Khalid	d. 1903	Died in infancy.
Faisal	1904-75	Foreign Minister from 1919; Viceroy of Hijaz 1926-53; proclaimed crown prince November 9, 1953; proclaimed king November 3, 1964; assassinated March 25, 1975.
Fahad	d. 1919	Born soon after Faisal.
Muhammad	1910-88	Commander of army which took the surrender of Medina 1925; renounced succession in 1965.
Khalid	1912-82	Proclaimed crown prince 1965; proclaimed king March 25, 1975.
Sa'ad	1914-19	Son of Hassa bint Ahmad Sudairi by her first marriage to Abdul Aziz.
Nasir	1920-84	Governor of Riyadh until 1947; stood down from succession in March 1975.
Sa'ad	1920-93	Son of Jauhara bint Sa'ad al- Sudairi, widow of Abdul Aziz's brother Sa'ad; stood down from succession in March 1975.
Fahad	1921-	First son of Hassa Sudairi after her remarriage to Abdul Aziz; Minister of Education, 1953-60; Interior Minister, 1962-75; Second Deputy Premier 1968-75; proclaimed crown prince March 25, 1975; King June 12, 1982.
Mansour	1922-51	Kingdom's first Minister of Defense, from 1944 till death.
Abdullah	1923-	Commander of National Guard 1963 to present day; Second Deputy Premier March 1975; Crown Prince June 1982.

First name	Dates	Career
Bandar	1923-	Noted for especially strict religious observance.
Musa'id	1923-	
Abdul Mohsen	1925-85	Last child of Jauhara Sudairi, widow of Abdul Aziz's brother Sa'ad; Minister of the Interior 1961-2; his son Sa'ud bin Abdul Mohsen is Deputy Governor of Mecca.
Misha'al	1925-	Minister of Defense 1951-5; one time Governor of Mecca.
Sultan	1927-	Minister of Communications, 1954-60; Minister of Defense and Aviation since 1962.
Miteib	1928-	Minister of Housing and Public Works since 1975.
Talal	1930-1	Died in infancy.
Abdul Rahman	1931-	Deputy Minister of Defense and Aviation since 1982.
Badr	d. 1931	Died in infancy.
Talal	1931-	Minister of Communications, 1953-4; Minister of Finance, 1960-1 Special Envoy, UNESCO, since 1979.
Mishari	1932-	
Turki	1933-	Vice-Minister of Defense until 1978.
Badr	1933-	Minister of Communications 1961-2; Deputy Commander of the National Guard.
Nawwaf	1933-	Special advisor on Gulf Affairs to King Faisal.
Naif	1934-	Former Governor of Riyadh; Interior Minister since 1975.
Fawwaz	1934-	Resigned as Governor of Mecca in December 1979.
Majid	1934-6	Died in childhood.
Salman	1936-	Governor of Riyadh since 1962.
Majid	1936-	Minister of Municipalities 1975-8; Governor of Mecca 1980.
Thamir	1937-58	Died in the reign of King Sa'ud.
Abdulillah	1938-	Governor of Qaseem until 1992.

First name	Dates	Career
Abdul Majeed	1940-	Governor of Medina since 1986.
Sattam	1940-	Deputy Governor of Riyadh.
Ahmad	1940-	Deputy Governor of Mecca 1975-8; Vice-Minister of Interior 1978.
Mamduh	1941-	Chairman of the Center for Strategic Studies in Riyadh.
Hidhlul	1941-	Business Interests.
Mashhur	1942-	Business Interests.
Abdul Salaam	1942-4	Died in childhood.
Muqrin	1943-	Former Saudi Air Force pilot; Governor of Hail 1980.
Hamoud	1947-	Business Interests.

Name and Subject Index

AKY1601 4.26.984 Puee